Do You Now Believe?

Do You Now Believe?

Reasonable Faith in Mark and John

PAMELA E. HEDRICK

☙PICKWICK *Publications* · Eugene, Oregon

DO YOU NOW BELIEVE?
Reasonable Faith in Mark and John

Copyright © 2017 Pamela E. Hedrick. All rights reserved. Except for brief quotations in critical publications or reviews, no part of this book may be reproduced in any manner without prior written permission from the publisher. Write: Permissions, Wipf and Stock Publishers, 199 W. 8th Ave., Suite 3, Eugene, OR 97401.

Pickwick Publications
An Imprint of Wipf and Stock Publishers
199 W. 8th Ave., Suite 3
Eugene, OR 97401

www.wipfandstock.com

PAPERBACK ISBN: 978-1-6109-7786-9
HARDCOVER ISBN: 978-1-4982-8659-6
EBOOK ISBN: 978-1-4982-4609-5

Cataloging-in-Publication data:

Names: Hedrick, Pamela E., author.

Title: Do you now believe? : reasonable faith in Mark and John / Pamela E. Hedrick.

Description: Eugene, OR: Pickwick Publications, 2017 | Includes bibliographical references.

Identifiers: ISBN: 978-1-6109-7786-9 (paperback) | ISBN: 978-1-4982-8659-6 (hardcover) | ISBN: 978-1-4982-4609-5 (ebook)

Subjects: LCSH: Faith—Biblical teaching | Bible. New Testament—Gospels. | Bibe. New Testament—Theology.

Classification: BS2585.2 H33 2017 (print) | BS2585.2 (ebook).

Manufactured in the U.S.A.   04/24/17

Scripture quotations are from the New Revised Standard Version Bible, copyright © 1989 National Council of the Churches of Christ in the United States of America. Used by permission. All rights reserved worldwide.

To Dave

Contents

Introduction | ix
1 The Reasonableness of Belief | 1
2 The Gospel of Mark | 17
3 The Gospel of John | 42
4 After Easter: The Application | 64
Conclusion | 76

Bibliography | 79

Introduction

"Blind faith" is a contentious phrase in contemporary Christianity. For those who champion it against what they see as a destructive modernism, it is a metaphorical call to arms.¹ For others, it is at best a mistaken understanding of the New Testament roots of the religion and at worst an insult to genuine religious belief. Many of our committed Christian students for decades have argued for a wide breach between what can be shown with evidence versus what must be acknowledged by faith; when pressed, they admit that by faith, they mean that which one believes without any evidence, and they usually insist on the necessity of "blind faith," generally ignoring the fact that even when they profess that so-called blind faith, they cannot seem to keep themselves from continuing to ask questions about it.

The first-century roots of Christianity are not immune to this controversy: the role of "faith" or "belief" in ancient Roman religion,² including the religion of the New Testament, has been a source of debate over the recent decades as well. Some insist that to speak of Roman "faith" or "belief" or even "religion" completely misreads paganism through the lens of Christianity, while others more recently have suggested that the trajectory of insisting on no

---

1. Or sometimes it serves as a purported reason to be morally and religiously opposed to reading their textbook.

2. Rather than repeating the term "Greco-Roman" each time, we will assume the profound influence of Greek religion on the Roman religions of the first century.

"faith" or "belief" in these religions has gone too far as a reaction against the Christian paradigm and have in their own way veiled important aspects of Roman religion.[3] In a sophisticated, complex, and nuanced analysis of Roman religion, one which is a substantial contribution to the field, Clifford Ando argues that Roman paganism was "empirically based" because it used sense data garnered through experimentation, and on that basis discarded what was not demonstrably efficacious. "For what we need urgently to understand is what the Romans had if not faith. The simple answer is: knowledge . . . Roman religion was thus founded upon an empiricist epistemology: cult addressed problems in the real world, and the effectiveness of rituals—their tangible results—determined whether they were repeated, modified, or abandoned."[4] Ando's insight here is a valuable one: just because the data does not pass our twenty-first century standards of evidence does not mean that the evidence was not empirical for the first-century participants, who of course had different standards of legitimation. Does, however, his juxtaposition of these pagan religions with Christianity, as well as the characterization of the Romans as "not having faith," hold water? Again, it depends on the definition of faith. For Ando, it is an idea held to be true without supporting evidence or verification. "Similarly, the correlative to pagan denunciations of Christian credulity (their religion was based on belief!) was again confidence that their practice was based on historical evidence."[5] Does the Christian apologetic rhetoric he cites from the fourth century, we might also ask, apply to the first century?

It seems clear that the supposed wide breach between Roman religion and Christianity (similar to another breach that some would argue is not reconcilable, modern science and Christianity) to a large part depends on how one defines "faith" and the process that leads to it. There is a sometimes subtle, sometimes not so subtle, assumption that faith is what comes into play when

---

3. A helpful and recent discussion can be found in Rives, *Religion*, 4–7; 13–53 and in the introduction by Ando, *Roman*, 1–14.

4. Ando, *Matter*, 13.

5. Ibid. 14.

all evidence is lacking. Is that true in, for example, any religious system in the Roman Empire during the first century? Is it ever true? Is the choice always faith or reason? Or, in the words of John Henry Newman, is faith "certainly an exercise of reason"?[6]

Even the word "evidence" is problematic. Does it refer to something "out there" in the external world? Or is it synonymous with "reasons," as in "I have good reasons for thinking that x?" Within the horizon of Anglo-American empiricism, for example, evidence is sometimes taken to mean what is out there, merely extrinsic evidence. In the stories about Jesus, extrinsic evidence would be something like walking on water, a healing or reading someone's thoughts. Reasons, however, seem to connote for most people a broader and subtler form of justification for belief. Too rarely do religious people have the benefit of understanding what it means to verify and then express their religious experience, so they fall back on mere assertions that will not be of interest to those listeners who would indeed like to understand the foundations of religious faith. Religious people often fail to express their experience in a way that seems reasonable to others. They can have good reasons for their belief without being able to communicate them.

The argument of this book is that the writings of the New Testament encourage transformation not through some magical blind faith but through a process of questioning that promotes a reasonable interpretation of experience, belief, conversion and transformation. The head and the heart, to use popular images, are inseparably engaged. Human beings hold beliefs based on evidence that they find convincing; our examples from Scripture of that fact will illustrate the dynamic role of the questions that constitute self-transcendence. But human living is never without its concrete context, and so we will take note of what the sociologist of knowledge Peter Berger call the "legitimations" that make reasonable the reception of the divine benefits and moral transformations that are witnessed in the Gospels and Acts.[7] In Chapter

---

6. Newman, "Nature," 207.

7. As we shall see later in this chapter, the terms "divine benefits" and "moral transformation" as we are using them come from Johnson, *Among the*

Introduction

1, arguments from theologian Bernard Lonergan, as well as social anthropologist Victor Turner, sociologist Peter L. Berger, and New Testament scholar Luke Timothy Johnson will provide a foundation for examining the reasonableness of belief that we find dramatized in the gospel narratives. In Chapter 2 we will apply those lessons to encounters in the Gospel of Mark, and in Chapter 3 to the Gospel of John. The final chapter contains considerations of how these conclusions about the dynamic of questioning headed toward a reasonable faith might apply to Christian experience in our contemporary world in light of Lonergan's transcendental precepts: be attentive, be intelligent, be reasonable, be responsible, be in love, and if necessary, change.

Gentiles.

1
The Reasonableness of Belief

The Foundations:
Understanding, Judgment, and Reasonable Faith

How then do we begin to demonstrate the reasonableness of belief, both in our modern culture and in the first century? The challenges from some post-Enlightenment philosophers have raised the issue in ways that are still influencing the debate. In the nineteenth-century Anglo-Saxon philosophical tradition, for example, it was widely taken for granted that John Locke was correct in thinking that when one assents to the truth of a proposition, that assent was a matter of degree. Assent was not only dependent upon evidence but also dependent for its strength on the degree of available evidence. Locke thought, and many still think, that if you have "weak" evidence, then you have a weak assent, and if you have "strong" evidence, then you have a strong assent.[1] His position gave rise in the late nineteenthth century to the "ethics of belief" debate in which some Lockean thinkers declared that it is not only irrational but potentially immoral for one to hold a belief that lacked an appropriate degree of evidence.[2] John Henry Newman begged to differ, and his work in *Grammar of Assent* thus helped set the stage in the next century for Bernard Lonergan's

---

1. Locke, *Human Understanding*, 15.
2. For a survey of the issues, see McCarthy, *Ethics*.

analysis of human cognition, which includes an important role for what we are calling "reasonable faith."[3]

For Newman, there is a very clear and verifiable distinction between *understanding* (which he also called "apprehension") and *judgment* (which he usually calls *assent*). Newman insisted that assent or its opposite is a "yes" or a "no" answer to a yes or no question,[4] and such questions allow for only three potential answers: assent, dissent, or doubt. Assent, in other words, is not an apprehension but an affirmation or negation of an apprehension. Nor is assent a matter of degree, as is apprehension; yes-or-no does not admit of degrees. To the objection that there are too many issues about which we are uncertain to make Newman's argument a reasonable one, Newman emphasizes "probability." But probability is on the level of apprehension or understanding, not on the level of assent,[5] and in fact, most of our knowledge is the product of affirmations of probabilities. For example, imagine that a patient has been told by her doctor that the medical literature indicates that 80% of the time her symptoms point to a particular medical problem. The physician has affirmed the 80%, but that affirmation (or assent or judgment) is not 80%; the judgment is simply an affirmation, a claim, a "yes" to the (unspoken) question, "Does the literature—yes or no—indicate that 80% of the time the symptoms express X?" Other than this affirmation, the doctor's judgment could only have been one of two other options: "No, the probability is not 80%," or "I don't really know what the probabilities are in this case." But the physician will make no sense if she says, "I'm probably saying that you probably have this disease." Probable judgments are affirmations of probabilities; they are not degrees of affirmation, which does not admit of degrees.

Understanding or apprehension, what calls forth a judgment regarding its veracity, is often less or more probable and so judgment is often to a probability. Newman spends a great deal of time in the *Grammar* discussing probability in order to indicate that it

3. Lonergan, *Method*, 41–47; Lonergan, *Insight*, 703–18.
4. Newman, *Grammar*, 110–11.
5. Ibid., 187–89.

is our understanding that admits of degrees, that we understand things to some degree or another, and rarely completely. What is being affirmed can be more or less well understood, but the effort to understand X, which results in some level or degree of understanding, can be affirmed and an affirmation is not a matter of degree.

Bernard Lonergan's notion of the "self-affirmation of the knower" brings us more explicitly to the "turn to the subject" that we find implicit in Newman.[6] For Lonergan, when one knows oneself and what one is doing when one is knowing, then one is on a sure footing for correctly understanding other acts of understanding and judgment. The claims about degrees of assent made by the Lockean writers involved in the "Ethics of Belief" debate can be corrected by an accurate grasp of the basic operations of cognition. The problem is solved not by proposing ideas but by understanding oneself. When we correctly affirm what it is that we do when we know, then the debate can be settled by empirical verification. In an effort to systematize the informal phenomenology of human cognition that we find in Newman, Lonergan picks up Newman's common sense distinction between apprehension and assent (in Lonergan's words, understanding and judgment) and makes it systematic. Most human assents or judgments are matters of belief; we accept on the word of another or others. Lonergan's most extensive analysis of the role of belief is in *Insight*;[7] he treats the topic more succinctly in *Method in Theology*.[8] For Lonergan, the distinction between "immanently generated knowledge" and "belief," and the importance of both, is crucial to delineate the distinction between understanding and judgment. Immanently generated knowledge means what I discover for myself (experience) rather than relying on someone else's testimony or other reasons. If one drives into a strange town looking for the library, one would find one's destination by reasonably relying on belief by asking someone the location, believing what one is told, and following those directions.

6. Lonergan, *Insight*, 319–47.
7. Ibid., 703–18.
8. Lonergan, *Method*, 41–46.

Once you get to the library, however, one has immanently generated knowledge: one knows for oneself how to get to that library.

But what about beliefs that cannot be so directly verified? Newman's famous example is his belief that "England is an island." How does he know that it is in fact an island? What's the evidence that he has? It is clear that this bit of knowledge is a belief rather than immanently generated knowledge. Few have sailed around it and mapped it for themselves. Yet, *it is not irrational to believe that England is an island; there are plenty of good reasons for that belief.* It would in fact be irrational not to believe it. And many of those reasons are themselves reasonable beliefs, such as one's confidence in maps, historical accounts, etc. A New Testament example of belief that becomes self-generated knowledge is the behavior of the Samaritan townspeople in the Fourth Gospel: they first believed on the basis of the woman's testimony, then saw for themselves and thus had immanently generated knowledge (John 4:39–42). (We shall return to this example.) But whether one's belief is later transformed into self-generated knowledge or not, the role of belief is ubiquitous and humanly inescapable.

Judgment and belief are personal operations and so individual differences will influence what will be considered as worthy of belief. A certain amount of evidence might convince one person but not another. Evidence, Lonergan emphasizes, is not what convinces us by necessity but by supplying all that we need to answer all of the relevant questions that need to be asked before the judgment is secure. The real is not "out there" to be seen but what is known in correct judgment, and so it is more accurate to say that *people* are convinced rather than that some evidence is convincing. Evidence can hardly be convincing without consideration of the person being convinced. Examples are easy to bring to mind: juries provide well-known examples, especially in their dramatized versions, such as the famous film *Twelve Angry Men*. The New Testament is rife with such examples, of course; one thinks of the many who left the scene described in John 6, while a few managed to stay, convinced that something special was or at least might be going to happen. The fact, however, that different evidence is convincing (or not) to different people does not make believing *per se* irrational. But it does highlight the locus of knowledge and belief in the subject and not in a formula regarding the degrees of evidence. The process of raising questions for understanding, for truth and for decision dynamically orients the subject beyond his or her present knowledge and commitments. We will use the term "self-transcendence" to identify the successful outcome of this process.

The Social Aspect of Knowledge

There are two basic types of data narrated in the New Testament as evidence of the truth of the gospel message: external or internal. A physical healing is an example of external data. The disciples on the road to Emmaus, whose hearts burned in them as Jesus interpreted the Scriptures (Luke 24:32), is an example of internal data. Internal experience, however, is sometimes discounted as evidence; some believers and some unbelievers have objected to internal evidence. Believers influenced by an older Christian apologetic look to miracles and prophecies—external evidence—as the more convincing and secure foundation for judgment. Skeptics persuaded by a rationalist or empiricist approach also look to the external evidence, but find it to be largely absent. The approach that we are taking in this book, however, holds that the dismissal of internal experience is often a function of a mistaken judgment of what is real. If the real is necessarily a physical body out there in the world, such as a miraculous violation of the laws of nature or a prophecy fulfilled in Jesus, then internal experiences such as insights, decisions, and love are not evidence. But if the real is what is understood and correctly affirmed in judgment, then an insight is just as real as water become wine.

Personal, internal evidence, however, is not merely private. Most human knowledge is belief rather than what is immanently generated experience, and as such it has a social character. We depend on the social dimension of knowledge, for example, every time we use a map of any sort. Natural science would never make progress if each scientist considered it an obligation of scientific method to demonstrate with immanently generated knowledge all that must be assumed before proceeding with an experiment. For science to advance, there are judgments that any scientist must accept on what she considers reliable testimony from the past and present. The chemist's belief in the periodic table is reasonable, legitimated by the clear irrationality of any refusal to accept the testimony concerning the antecedent discoveries of previous scientists. Human knowledge, moreover has an historical character: progress in knowledge has occurred only because the next researchers began where predecessors left off, and they could do so only because they had *enough* evidence of a particular sort that they made the judgment of value to believe. Relying only on one's own experience would create an impossible situation of always beginning afresh and send us back to the stone age. Instead, we rely on a "common fund" of knowledge that we find reasonable to believe. When we find some aspect of that fund to be unreasonable, we stop believing it, begin to doubt it and move to verify that our doubts are justified. "A man does not learn without the use of his own senses, his own mind, his own heart, yet not exclusively by these."[9] One makes a free and responsible judgment on the value of deciding to believe that some proposition is probably or certainly true or false. All people, whether aware of it or not, are motivated by some good to be achieved by collaborating in the pursuit of truth by believing.

Having a common fund of knowledge is, of course, no *guarantee* that that knowledge is true; belief must be analyzed for mistakes of limitation and of bias. Hence, the importance of ongoing questioning. A judgment is, in Lonergan's terms, a "virtually unconditioned" operation of conciousness.[10] The conditions are fulfilled when there are no more relevant questions to be raised and answered. But often there *are* further relevant questions, whether known at the time of the judgment or not, and so one can speak of "probable judgments." These are judgments that, as Lonergan says, converge on an absolute but do not achieve it.

9. Lonergan, *Method*, 43.
10. Ibid., 44.

> The self-correcting process of learning consists in a sequence of questions, insights, further questions, and further insights that moves towards a limit in which no further, pertinent questions arise. When we are well beyond that limit judgments are obviously certain. When we are well short of that limit, judgments are at best probable. When we are on the borderline, the rash are completely certain and the indecisive full of doubts. In brief, because the self-correcting process of learning is an approach to a limit of no further, pertinent questions, there are probable judgments that are probably true in the sense that they approximate to a truth that as yet is not known.[11]

What Lonergan calls the "self-correcting process of learning" expresses the fact that further relevant questions are critically important for progress in knowledge. It also reveals that we can only speak of progress if our correct understandings converge toward a goal.

The common fund of knowledge typically suffers from certain distortions in our knowing, and that imperfection is why belief is often held in low regard. Those who are preoccupied with necessary knowledge are especially doubtful. We have known since Socrates' confrontation with the Sophists that convention is no guarantee of truth. The remedy, Lonergan says, is not rejection of belief but a critical intelligence that selflessly seeks the truth and thereby promotes progress and offsets decline. Evaluating the source of the belief is a critical step. The source may be in error, or the mistake could be a result of a limitation of one's own intellectual, moral or religious horizon that blocks understanding. To cite a familiar biblical example, the Gospel of John makes use of the limitation of horizons when characters such as Nicodemus take Jesus' words literally rather than symbolically (John 3:1–10).

In the process of making a judgment to believe, if the evaluation leaves no further relevant questions at the moment and in the particular context, then one can reasonably decide to believe. She has decided that the assertion is credible as well as valuable

---

11. Lonergan, *Insight*, 300.

if it is believed, and so it should be believed. A final step follows, which Lonergan calls the "act of believing," which also entails the responsibility to add that knowledge to the common fund.

How can this analysis of the structure of consciousness and its social implications apply to our topic on the reasonableness of the earliest Christianity witnessed to in the documents preserved in the New Testament? Lonergan's most basic achievement has been to show that all new knowledge is the result of the invariant structure of consciousness that raises questions for understanding our experience and then asks the further question for reflection to determine whether that understanding is correct, or probably so. If we assume that the structure of human consciousness is universal and invariant—the "rock" on which a critically realist epistemology can be built—then we can hope to understand the process of belief and reasonableness in ancient and all other cultures. Lonergan's theory of belief is bolstered by the way belief and legitimation are treated within the sociology of knowledge, especially as it attends to religious systems. Various times and cultures hold differing legitimations but the structure of legitimation and belief is the same. So the question is not, "what are the necessary and universal legitimations that would warrant belief" but rather "what constitutes evidence in a given socio-historical situation?" In order to answer that question, one is inevitably involved in an historically conscious sociology of knowledge.

Social Systems and the Role of Experience

Peter L. Berger discusses religion's function as a system that serves to maintain the social order by identifying it with cosmic order. Since religions are symbol systems, they serve as legitimations in different ways according to their specific historical and cultural settings. By legitimation "is meant the socially objectivated 'knowledge' that serves to explain and justify the social order."[12] For our purposes, it is essential to note that "the historically crucial

---

12. Berger, *Sacred Canopy*, 29.

part of religion in the process of legitimation is explicable in terms of the unique capacity of religion to 'locate' human phenomena within a cosmic frame of reference."[13] Thus, religions located in the same time and region that confidently claim universal knowledge tend to have profound similarities.

Of course they also manifest differences because, although they share a great number of cultural presuppositions, people are not simply the automatic products of socialization. Though legitimations are human products, they also come to have a kind of autonomy and authority, so that they can affect the society as well in a dialectical process: they are human products while at the same time producing human products such as beliefs.[14] In order to maintain the beliefs that one is socialized into, there must be legitimations; in some broad sense there must be convincing evidence of the truth that is proposed if they are to be accepted as reasonable. If beliefs are not legitimized and thus held to be legitimate—in other words, if legitimations fail—then people look elsewhere for answers to basic questions. To pretend we can operate otherwise, "exempted from the process variously named socialization and acculturation" would be to ignore our historicity.[15]

Early Christianity developed in the Greco-Roman world, and therefore it depended *at that time* on similar types of legitimations as other contemporary religions. What served to legitimate Christianity is in part rooted in its Romanness: Christians were first-century people living within smaller cultures subsumed to greater and lesser degrees under the larger culture of the Roman Empire. The differences narrow between Christianity and other Roman religions when the question regards the activity and presence of the divine in some discernible manner. There are examples in ancient Christianity and some other ancient Mediterranean religious texts of the experience of the divine that reveals the benefits of belief, such as healings as witnessed to in the New Testament and in inscriptions from sanctuaries of Asclepius. The evangelists, that is,

13. Ibid., 35.
14. Ibid., 40.
15. Lonergan, *Method*, 223.

expressed how in the early communities their experience of Jesus validated and strengthened some traditional Roman legitimations but also corrected and advanced others.

Uncovering Reasonableness

Challenges abound with regard to our topic of reasonableness of belief, whether we examine those religions traditionally called "pagan" or Jewish or the early Christian movement that developed within and from Judaism. The study of Roman religion has been plagued not only by Christian bias but also by a subsequent reaction against the Christian bias, yielding similarly distorted views. Problems with the study of earliest Christianity in its religious context are also plentiful, especially when we compare Christianity with other religions in their cultural contexts. For example, stereotypes of a uniform and elitist Christianity have often colored research on both sides. Those stereotypes often arise from considering only a later, hierarchical and highly organized form of Christianity, or from the western Protestant perspective and its reaction against both hierarchy and sacramental views of Catholicism, or from the perspective of some who consider Christianity more as a set of dogmas (including some Christians themselves!) than as lived experiences that engage intellectual and moral exigencies. While it can be useful in some contexts to discern the difference between Greco-Roman religion and a European-American-Protestant Christian stereotype of religion, it is not useful when considering first-century Christianity, which only rarely, locally, and late in the century had a highly structured form of authority, an emphasis on written texts and developed dogma. Rather, earliest Christianity sought knowledge of a god and of that god's will, looked for distinct evidence of it, acted when they thought they understood it, had confidence based on what they considered historical evidence, but were willing to alter their view based on new experiential evidence; in other words, generally similar to the way Clifford

Ando describes the way Roman religion operated.[16] The Christian conclusions regarding the reasonableness of this empirical data, in other words, are based on experience—one's own and that of others (healing, for example)—as well as personal or communal renewal coming from divine benefits.

In other words, we are in the realm of Berger's description of legitimations of the social/religious order as well as the reasonableness of belief as suggested by Newman and Lonergan. Divine activity, practitioners believed, took place in a discernible manner that one would grasp through observation of patterns, both present and historical, of matters that turned out well, or not. That evidence led them to believe that they understood the presence and activities of the gods well *enough* to believe in the gods, participate in religious practices and reap both personal and communal benefits (physical, spiritual, ethical). If there are conflicts in that evidence, the more recent evidence trumps the older. That practice of communicating with the power and presence of the gods led often to expansions of the inherited religious beliefs/practices as the knowledge was communicated into the common fund of knowledge. In other words, their search for meaning was a reasonable one, carried out by reasonable means according to the standards of legitimation at that time.

The pattern that Ando finds in Roman religion has parallels to recent work by Luke Timothy Johnson, who has considerably advanced comparative study that avoids previous pitfalls. In *Among the Gentiles: Greco-Roman Religion and Christianity*, Johnson identifies four types of religiosity in Greco-Roman religion and argues for the presence of two of those four in early Christianity: (A) participation in divine benefits, and (B) moral transformation. When participation in divine benefits is the primary type, the texts give evidence of religious practitioners' focus on discerning the presence and powerful activity of divine *dynamis* (power) in the world. Whether through sacrifices, prayers, prophecies, healings, mysteries or pilgrimages (usually a combination of several), the goal is to gain access to that power and its effects on humans.

16. Ando, *Matter*, 3–15.

"This mode of religiosity is optimistic about the empirical world as the arena of divine activity. It is intensely pragmatic about the benefits the gods offer: salvation involves security and success in this mortal life."[17] Johnson examines Aelius Aristides' *Sacred Tales* to show in detail the operation of this religiosity that seeks access to the divine *dynamis* and the benefits one can gain through participation in it. The four canonical gospels in particular participate in this "Religiousness A."

What Johnson calls "Religiousness B" is religion as moral transformation, in which "the most important activity of the divine power is perceived as immanent within human moral endeavor, and 'salvation' is less a matter of divine rescue from human failure and disaster than the ability of humans to endure such circumstances in a manner worthy of the gods."[18] An examination of Epictetus' *Discourses* shows that those who fall into this type certainly do not deny the practices and divine power associated with Religiousness A; rather, their focus is almost exclusively on the particular locus of that power "within human activity and expressed through moral transformation."[19] Johnson considers Paul as the primary example in the New Testament of this type of religiosity.

Ando, Johnson, and indeed Lonergan all recognize structures of human living; Lonergan, however, gives far more attention to the universal and therefore necessary process of reasonable reflection on what the subject perceives as experience of divine power.[20] These structures function as the generalized anthropological presuppositions brought to the interpretation of religion. Although fully aware of the historicity of human thought, Lonergan's "generalized empirical method" lays out the operations of the human

17. Johnson, *Among the Gentiles*, 50.
18. Ibid., 64.
19. Ibid., 77.
20. Consider, for example, Joachim Wach's important essay "The Nature of Religious Experience." He defined typical aspects of religious experience without due attention to the cognitive processes that are necessary to appropriating and acting on what is learned from the experience. We could add more examples from work on religious experience by phenomenologists.

mind that can be found throughout human history. The method is *generalized* because it is operating whenever one is thinking; it is not discipline specific. It is *empirical* because it starts not with abstractions but with the actual operations of the mind. It is a *method*, not in the sense of a recipe or rote formula, but in the sense that one is able to examine critically any form of argument by locating the basic and unavoidable operations of experience, understanding, judgment and decision.

We recognize its elements long before Lonergan systematized them, of course. In a very general and unsystematic sense, what Lonergan called cognition is what Aristotle called *phronesis*, Aquinas called intellect, and Newman called the illative sense. The epigraph to *Insight* is a quotation from Aristotle's *De Anima* (III, 7, 431b 2): "The mind, in the image, grasps form." The point of commonality among these philosophers of intelligence is that, prior to any sort of concept, logic, argument, or discursive reasoning, there is the insight. The cognitional event that Lonergan calls insight, in other words, was known in the ancient world; Aristotle called it *eidos* or *morphē* (form). Even apart from Aristotle's formulation of it, the event is simply a common human occurrence. And so, even though we are using Lonergan's terminology as the best theoretical articulation of the basic cognitional operations of the human mind, we are not imposing a modern experience onto ancient minds.

Because the New Testament was written by human beings, we see the process there as well. In his article "Transformation of the Mind and Moral Discernment in Paul," Johnson recognizes the role of transformation in Aristotle's treatment of the *nous* (mind) and applies it to Paul's pneumatological and christological expansion in Romans. "In Plato as in Aristotle, the capacity to 'test' or 'estimate' morally derives from the *nous*, not simply intellect as a capacity, but perhaps something closer to what we would call a 'mind-set,' that is a moral intelligence that grasps certain fundamental principles or values. In Plato and in Aristotle, the corruption of the *nous* makes moral discernment impossible rather than simply difficult."[21] Paul's distinctive turn is to claim that those who are "in Christ" are using not only their own human prudential reasoning but that of Christ as well ("the mind of Christ"), with the Holy Spirit enabling the "capacity to see truly and act appropriately."[22] The point is the good of community, which is the body of Christ, as well as the individual member. "The measure of sound moral reasoning is not hitting the mean which is virtue but corresponding to the faith of Christ which is spelled out in lowly service to others. In short, the habits Paul seeks to shape in his readers are the habits of Jesus, the character he seeks to mold in his communities is the character of Jesus."[23]

We find Johnson's insights in this vein persuasive, and we would like to complement his work and hope to advance the issue by means of an approach that finds compatible results, with an eye to application within our present understanding and experience of Christianity. We will, however, use a different mode of inquiry to uncover this same development but in a different genre than Paul's letters, i.e. in the gospel narratives. We maintain that the stories in the gospels of Mark and John often narrate the process of *questioning* to demonstrate that participation in divine benefits and especially moral transformation are reasonable evidence for belief.

The very fact of questioning is the most obvious evidence for the human quest for meaning. Questions imply answers, and the answers that many of the characters in religious texts seek matter to them. The answers help determine the "should" and "ought" of decision and potential action. In *Theology of the Christian Word: A Study in History*, Lonergan scholar Frederick E. Crowe points out that "[t]he quest for understanding is expressed, quite fittingly, in questions,"[24] then he carefully elucidates both the types of questions we ask and the importance of recognizing this same process of questioning in Greco-Roman religiosity and the narratives of the New Testament. Faced with an experience, we observe

21. Johnson, "Transformation," 160.
22. Ibid., 235.
23. Ibid., 235–36.
24. Crowe, *Theology*, 83.

The Reasonableness of Belief

ourselves asking three types of questions. First are questions for understanding, "what, why, and how" questions, as when Mary of Nazareth asks, "How can this be, since I am a virgin?" (Luke 1:34). Answers to questions for understanding prompt the second type, questions for reflection on the truth of one's understanding. These answers respond to "yes or no" questions and issue in judgments about whether something is or is not so. Is the idea you have true? Is it knowledge? Or is it merely an idea? In Matthew 11:3 John the Baptist sends from prison the question regarding Jesus: "Are you the one who is to come, or are we to wait for another?" John suspects but does not yet know that Jesus is the one who is to come. Third, we see questions for deliberation about what to do based on this knowledge, questions regarding the value and goodness of a course of action, as when the crowds ask in response to John the Baptist's preaching: "What then should we do?" (Luke 3:10).[25] Questions sometimes appear, of course, as more implicit than explicit; for example, "the people were on the tiptoe of expectation, all wondering about John, whether perhaps he was the Messiah" (Luke 3:15).[26] Crowe pointedly notes that it is not just his "Catholic piety toward Mary that convinces [him] it was not her hardness of heart that made her slow to understand."[27] "Surely there is question of an object that is hidden, mysterious, hard to fathom, question too of a mental activity of wondering, debating, supposing, and reflecting, and question finally of a breakthrough to an insight that combines intelligence and understanding with religious experience."[28]

In this study, we do not seek new overall interpretations of these two gospels. We will, rather, examine both explicit and implicit questions particularly in the gospels of Mark and John to bring to light this common activity of reasonable faith leading, ideally, toward a new way of seeing and acting in the world. We will argue that what Lonergan calls "conceptualism" is the obstacle

25. Ibid., 46–47.
26. Ibid., 46.
27. Ibid., 86.
28. Ibid.

that links all those characters in the four gospels who do not understand Jesus.[29] Conceptualism is the failure to notice that insight or understanding is more basic than concepts or their formulation. Concepts are abstract and detached from the data of experience. Understanding is the grasp of the intelligibility in the data of experience; when understanding is ignored and concepts are imposed on the data, then what is new in experience cannot be grasped. For example, in first-century Judaism, there were many different ways of thinking about the Messiah or the Messianic age. If one with a conceptualist mentality were to encounter Jesus, one would begin with an inherited concept of "messiah" and then judge Jesus according to the concept. But what if Jesus—and the experience of him—does not fit into the initial concept? Intelligence would require a return to the data of experience—what is Jesus saying and doing?—in an effort to understand the man himself. But if conceptualism wins out, Jesus will be misunderstood to the degree that he does not match the preconceived idea. To take another example, in the synoptic gospel story of the healing of the paralytic Jesus forgives sins, and so he is conceived as a blasphemer since no one can forgive sins but God (Mark 1:45—2:10; Matt 9:2–7; Luke 5:15–25). Insight requires that one approach experience without an already fixed concept that, one imagines, must fit the data. Attentive inquiry rather than concepts and their logical arrangement is the beginning of understanding. When those who encounter Jesus allow themselves to be amazed by Jesus, there is the potential for them to grasp the meaning of the man. Among other strategies, these gospels narrate scenes of questioning for the purpose of challenging the reader to a transformed way of thinking: *metanoia* (conversion). It is our hope that this study will help the reader to recognize in these New Testament modes of inquiry and legitimation potential paths to transformation for our own time and place.

---

29. Lonergan, *Method*, 74–75.

2

The Gospel of Mark

When looking for evidence of the reasonableness of belief in the earliest Christians or anyone else in the first century, it is necessary both to respect their experiences and to investigate how they reflected on them. We have seen that religious transformation happens not merely by *having* an experience but upon *reflection* on that experience. The meaning of the experience is legitimized in the transformation, confirming one's responsible acceptance of the religion's expressions of the truth. The meaning (or interpretation) of the experience and the personal response it enables can be judged to be reasonable or not, and therefore to be acted upon in a certain way or not. As also mentioned in the preceding chapter, in the first-century religious experience as communicated in the New Testament gospels functioned to provide access to the divine *dynamis*, opening the possibility of transformation. Johnson describes it well: "It is a power that comes from outside those touched by it and is transmitted to them from another, to whom it properly belongs. The power transmitted to them reaches external expression in various 'wonders and signs,' including healings and exorcisms and gifts of ecstatic speech. But it is also said to be at work in the internal transformation of human freedom."[1]

---

1. Johnson, *Religious Experience*, 7.

We suggest that in the Gospel of Mark an often overlooked area of reasonable reflection on the divine *dynamis* takes the form of explicit questioning on the part of Jesus, the disciples, and others around him. In this gospel, we hear questions for understanding (asking for meaning), questions for reflection (yes or no judgments about the truth of the meaning that is proposed for belief), and questions for deliberation (what then shall we do, given this true meaning). This evangelist shows that the dynamic of questioning can fall into several different patterns, for as Lonergan makes clear, it is not always a one-way street from experience to understanding to judgment. Often one discovers that one has inherited or believed something that is not the case. The error must then be purged. "For when one makes a discovery, when one comes to know what one did not know before, often enough one is advancing not merely from ignorance to truth but from error to truth. To follow up on such discovery is to scrutinize the error, to uncover other connected views that in one way or another supported or confirmed it. These associates of the error may themselves be errors. They will bear examination."[2]

The inevitability of believing, then, does not negate the need for a dynamic process of sorting through and purifying one's inherited beliefs. The goal of this process of inquiry is a going beyond the previous horizon of one's understanding of self and of God. The goal is self-transcendence.

That Jesus is more a man of actions than of words in Mark, at least more than in any other canonical gospel, is not in dispute.[3] His actions, however, which demonstrate the accessibility of the

---

2. Lonergan, *Method*, 44.

3. Rather than trying to sort out the historical Jesus from the proclaimed Jesus as two categories, we assume a creative tension of both/and; in other words, that the proclaimed Jesus is consistent enough with the historical Jesus in meaning. We assume that the canonical gospels reflect accurately the meaning of what Jesus said and did upon reflection by his earliest followers and their followers (and their followers after that), what we will call a bit anachronistically the early Christian community, those in the first century who believed that Jesus in some way played a definitive role in cosmic reality. Nonetheless, the gospels each present their own particular portrayal of Jesus, hence the "Markan Jesus," the "Johannine Jesus," etc.

divine *dynamis*, are often the end result of the answer to questions of deliberation: what is to be done? Jesus' response, often in action (miracles) but also in verbal teaching, reveals the new understanding of cosmic reality that the gospels call "the kingdom of God" (Mark 1:15, etc.). The patterns of the questioning process differ, because the Gospel reveals both the ways people succeed and also the ways they fail in appropriating the meaning of Jesus and the kingdom. Jesus sometimes initiates the questioning process, then answers; at other times, questioners initiate and Jesus informs or corrects to demonstrate to them what is reasonable belief and action in light of what they are experiencing in him.[4] It is interesting that, in a significant number of encounters, Jesus corrects their flawed initiation of the process of inquiry to give them the best hope of fully engaging a truer understanding of cosmic reality and the transformation of mind and action required to conform themselves to it. Fellow Jews listened to Jesus and realized that their previously assumed way of being loyal to Judaism could be changed or expanded; in other words, Jesus' interpretations opened a new understanding of how their continuing commitment to the covenant could be enhanced. But more often in the stories of this gospel, even when hit full in the face with clear evidence for the divine *dynamis* present in Jesus' actions and words, the narrative does not display definitive evidence of transformation in the questioners. Mark highlights their failure to ask the right question or accept Jesus' answers in order to demonstrate to the authorial audience[5] what is reasonable faith and what is not.

4. Luke Johnson argues that while "participation in divine benefits" is present throughout the gospels and Acts, "the decisive element of Religiousness B . . . is missing, namely, the perception of the divine *dynamis* being immanently present precisely in order to effect a moral transformation" (152). While it is helpful for purposes of discussion to distinguish A and B, with regard to B, that seems to be primarily a matter of degree. We do not wish to suggest a re-categorization but to point out the way the aspect of transformation in Mark is portrayed by means of the strategy of a questioning that presumes the full use of a reasonable pursuit of truth by Jesus and his desire to teach his followers this mindset as well.

5. The terms "narrative audience" and "authorial audience" will be used to denote the observers and listeners in the story versus the audience the

The dynamic of questioning when carried out properly, moreover, has an interesting pattern that parallels the ritual process highlighted particularly by anthropologists Arnold van Gennep and Victor Turner. To summarize briefly, the now-familiar structure as Turner delineated it, a change in status in traditional societies is carried out through a precise ritual process. This process first entails "separation" from the previous status and the group, symbolized in particular by a physical removal with those of the same status to a particular location away from the rest of society and under the guidance of a leader. The threshold or "liminality" stage of the ritual involves a potentially traumatic disintegration of the previous status without any new status yet apparent. Various symbols tend to encourage a commonality of experience among the initiands that Turner called *communitas*. The experience of this intermediate stage is also characterized by a similarity in "aggregation," which entails the re-entry into society with a new status.[6]

The process of questioning that is the engine of human consciousness in some ways parallels the experience of ritual process. A new and/or difficult experience to incorporate into socially objectivated knowledge (see Chapter 1) results in a question for understanding, a question asked from within the present situation but tending toward *separation* from a previously held understanding of the cosmic frame of reference. Questions for reflection, seeking a yes or no judgment about the veracity of the meaning, can issue in the loss of a kind of status. In other words, a struggle to release the previously held certainties and make room for new knowledge can throw one's understanding of the cosmic order and one's place in it into a kind of painful chaos or *liminality*. Questions for deliberation can then show the way toward an *aggregation*: how does one act upon this new knowledge that results in a new understanding of the cosmos and one's role in it?

The Markan Jesus shows himself early in the narrative to be a master of the questioning process. We see Jesus exhibiting the

author hoped would hear (or more rarely, read) the gospel. See Rabinowitz, "Whirl," 85.

6. Turner, *Ritual*.

universal pattern of the operations of human consciousness (understanding/reflection/deliberation), whether his questions are explicit or implicit. In other words, Jesus in Mark asks questions in order to convince his hearers that faith in the cosmic order—the kingdom of God—is a supremely reasonable and radically transformative faith. Or, we might put it this way: how does one, to put it in Johnson's terms, gain access to the divine *dynamis* and its benefits according to Mark? One does so not just by being present to Jesus but in following his leads to consider the meaningfulness and truth of the change in cosmic order that is manifest in Jesus' words and deeds, and then to take up one's proper role in that order.

With such "big bangs" of healing and nature miracles often concluding and thus upstaging the questioning process in Mark, however, it is easy and typical for readers to skip lightly over the crucial questioning that precedes them and the effects on the participants and onlookers that follow them. But as the passage regarding Beelzebub (Mark 3:22) shows, it is not the miracle itself that is definitive; rather, it is the understanding of it and the appropriation of its meaning that counts. Thus, in examining the different ways the process moves forward, or not, we will examine these passages according to their similar patterns of movement: ideal patterns that lead to transformation; patterns that leave hope for a transformation not explicitly stated; questioning processes corrected by Jesus with varying results, and processes frustrated for the characters in the narrative but still fruitful for the authorial audience.[7]

---

7. Because, again, we are not seeking a new interpretation of the gospel as a whole or specific motifs, we are not using a narrative process of moving through the gospel as an auditor would hear the entire work. There are many studies that do proceed that way with excellent results for the reader to consult. One of the best such short treatments, for example, remains that of Tannehill, "Disciples." In a related vein is the work of Joanna Dewey on Mark as performance (e.g., "Survival"). Our approach here, however, in some ways complements that of Tolbert, "Character," in which she examines "the typological nature" (4) of character depiction in the ancient Mediterranean in general and in Mark in particular.

Ideal Examples of the Questioning Process

Mark's narrative presents clearly the difficult challenges involved in understanding the cosmic order that Jesus comes to announce and embody. In keeping with that aspect of Mark, there are few instances of the completed ideal of the questioning process in the gospel, and even fewer of its issuing in obvious personal transformation. There are, however, a few instances in which the participant has *enough* reasonable evidence to engage this cosmic order and what it brings in the person and ministry of Jesus.

The first question of the gospel occurs early, in the initial teaching in the synagogue at Capernaum (1:21–29). Interestingly, it is the unclean spirit who cries out, "What have you to do with us, Jesus of Nazareth? Have you come to destroy us? I know who you are, the Holy One of God." Despite being a scriptural formula that leans toward rejecting commonality between the speaker and the addressee,[8] the first question provides at least an opening for understanding, while the second is a question for reflection. The statement "I know who you are" is the result of a correct judgment of value to the question for reflection: yes, you have come to destroy us because we have opposing value systems. The demon correctly answers his own questions: yes, Jesus has come to destroy the hold that Satan has on the world. What to do, a question for deliberation, is answered in Jesus' action, ordering the unclean spirit out, because what brings misery has no place in the healing God seeks to bring.

The demon's interrogation and Jesus' response bears fruit in evoking other questions from those present: "What is this?" That is the real purpose of the encounter in the narrative. Their own answer is the insight: it is a new, authoritative teaching that the unclean spirits obey. The cosmic reach of the *dynamis* is clear in its effects: separation (why are you here?), liminality (a Holy One who does not conform to the reigning system of evil) and aggregation (the act of exorcism, the only reasonable response in light of the cosmic reality Jesus seeks to teach and embody). The

---

8. Donahue, *Mark*, 80.

full process leads to recognition in the narrative's audience of an understanding of the cosmic order in which evil will be dismissed, a cosmic authority not attributed to the scribes (1:22). The common knowledge that powers of both good and evil are operative in the world has now expanded to include the experience of a man with no apparent cultural authority who is revealed to have more cosmic authority than respected leaders of the religion. Previous beliefs are corrected and new insights open an expanded horizon.

The pattern of reasonable questioning bears fruit in two other episodes, both occurring in the critical central section of the gospel. The first (9:14–29) is a masterful example of success wrapped in one of failure. Jesus asks a simple question for understanding: what are the crowd, his disciples, and some scribes arguing about? Upon hearing the description of the possessed boy whom the disciples could not help, Jesus moves to an exasperated question that is actually more of a warning than a genuine question for understanding: "You faithless generation, how much longer must I be among you? How much longer must I put up with you?" (9:19). In other words, understanding is important, you are not getting it, and the time is short, assuming there is "at least a hint of Jesus' own sense of his approaching death here."[9]

When the boy is brought to Jesus and convulses, the positive example begins. Jesus asks how long this has been happening, leading the father who brought the ill child to ask for help if Jesus is able. Jesus retorts that all things are possible with belief, and the man returns one of the most honest and reasonable lines in the gospels: "I believe; help my unbelief!" (9:24). The father has assessed the information available concerning Jesus and upon reflection has judged that Jesus can indeed help. Yet the man acknowledges that his understanding is limited: his belief in Jesus is not blind, or even complete, but it is enough to be effective: the evidence is *enough* for him to make a probable judgment that he should believe, despite the limitation that he acknowledges as his unbelief. Confirmation that the father's judgment was reasonable follows immediately as Jesus responds to this man's faith by

9. Ibid., 278.

healing the boy. The story affirms an honest process of questioning that leads to insight about oneself and the cosmic order that is at hand in Jesus.

Interestingly, this exclusively Markan story and a detailed one for this evangelist, concludes not here but wraps back around to the beginning of the pericope when the disciples ask why they could not exorcise the demon (9:28), a question for understanding but a lame and egocentric one that shows that, despite what they have seen, the disciples are still not moving forward in their understanding. Starkly, the evangelist here puts forward to the authorial audience the difference between transformation and its lack, between responsible belief that can expand one's horizon and bias that leaves one trapped. The problem is only compounded by the disciples' fearful silence in the face of Jesus second pronouncement of his death and resurrection.[10]

In the second fully fruitful situation in the center of the gospel, the character whom we see in the narrative being transformed through reasonable belief is Bartimaeus (10:46–52). The process here is also highlighted by a change of order. Only one question is explicit: "What do you want me to do for you?" (10:51). But implied in Bartimaeus' shouting for Jesus "Son of David, have mercy on me!" (10:47, 48) is already a faith based on some understanding of Jesus.[11] Bartimaeus has enough faith in Jesus now to ask aloud: "My teacher, let me see again" (10:51). One would assume that he makes this request through heightened listening about the way the divine *dynamis* has been apparent in Jesus' previous healings. The true cosmic order that Bartimaeus already believes in is demonstrated in Jesus' response. He heals Bartimaeus, who without hesitation answers the implicit question for deliberation and turns his life to the new order: "Immediately he regained his sight and

---

10. "On a narrative level, the disciples' reserve may partly be a response to what had occurred in 8:31–33, where Peter protested Jesus' first clear passion prediction, only to find himself, and by implication the rest of the Twelve, roundly rebuked by Jesus. The Markan disciples may not have become more enlightened since then, but they do seem to have become more gun-shy" (Marcus, *Mark 8–16*, 669).

11. Williams, *Other Followers*, 154.

followed him on the way" (10:52). He is the only character up to this point in the narrative, other than the disciples, to trust, understand, and choose to follow Jesus. "Bartimaeus, who believes, sees and follows, now exemplifies what it means to fulfill the demands of Jesus."[12]

The brevity of the exchange shows with clarity that reasonable belief bears fruit. The effect of this process of Jesus' question and Bartimaeus' response, followed by his being healed and transformed into a disciple, is only heightened by a previous story of the only other blind man in Mark (8:22–26). The necessity of a two-stage healing process for this passive ("some people brought"), anonymous ("a blind man"), and apparently doubtful recipient of Jesus' healing (the people begged Jesus, not the blind man) brings in the narrative only physical healing. One would not want to minimize that outcome for a literal sufferer, but in symbolic terms for the life of discipleship, its purpose seems (1) to indicate that seeing is possible, and (2) to point ahead and to lead the auditor to anticipate the more successful model of Bartimaeus,[13] because here, even though there is physical healing, there is no evidence of transforming insight for the character himself.

Hope for Transformation

In the situations of the pre-Jerusalem part of the Gospel that we have examined so far, Jesus demonstrates the response to questions for deliberation (what do we do?) through action that he intends to be imitated by the disciples. We actually only see transformation happening in these two cases, although in subsequent scenes there is hope (with some actual evidence) of personal transformation, acceptance of and seeking to participate in the cosmic order revealed by the divine *dynamis*. As the narrative moves closer to the crucifixion, however, these patterns of questioning are completed more often in explicit teaching than in active

---

12. Ibid., 164–66.
13. Ibid., 129.

Do You Now Believe?

demonstration and only leave the door open for transformation. In a series of encounters in which Jesus' teaching shows him to have greater authority than the religious establishment and even than Rome (11:27–12:44), for example, the hope is for the crowd who presumably has more understanding by which to judge righteous authority from unrighteous.

The deceitful intent of the Sadducees who question Jesus (12:18–27) is disclosed by the narrator when he reports that they do not believe in the resurrection, yet they try to trap Jesus in a question about it anyway (12:23). Jesus does not bother to straighten out their question but rather issues the judgment: "Is not this the reason you are wrong, that you know neither the scriptures nor the power of God?" He then returns to the truth of the resurrection: "He is God not of the dead, but of the living; you are quite wrong." The scribe's seemingly sincere question about the most important commandment (12:28–34), and his subsequent agreement with Jesus' answer about the two primary commandments, show a Jesus superior in judgment and practice (12:28–40). Even this story of an honest question for understanding is ultimately geared to demonstrate Jesus' rhetorical defeat of part of the Jerusalem establishment,[14] as are the tour-de-force Scripture demonstrations mocking the triumphalist Davidic ideology (12:35–37). it also sets up the question for deliberation and its answer: beware the scribes who seek ego gratification over service to God and others (12:38–40). This critique of the scribes is hardly a case of transformation accomplished, but it does raise optimism for such transformation in the Jesus' audience.

In the "little apocalypse" of 13:1–32, Jesus initiates the questioning with a rhetorical one: "Do you see these great buildings? Not one stone will be left here upon another; all will be thrown down" (13:2). After some apparent thought, Peter, James, John and Andrew are prompted to ask him more questions for understanding: "Tell us, when will this be, what will be the signs that all these things are about to be accomplished?" Jesus' long teaching about the apocalyptic signs answers questions for reflection (yes,

---

14. Santos, *Slave*, 219.

this will happen) and deliberation (do not believe all the claims of messianic identity, stay alert, and so on). The pattern continues of teaching rather than action, resolving the full range of answers, but since the exchange involves future events, there is only hope regarding successful effect (transformation) on the disciples, and that hope extends to the authorial audience.

Interestingly, one episode near the end of the gospel does show Jesus' answer to an implied question for deliberation in both his teaching and action: the Last Supper (14:17–25). The scene begins not with a question but by Jesus' statement that someone there would betray him. All ask, "Surely, not I?" (14:19), which could also be read as already having made the judgment, "No, not I." Jesus repeats the prediction and warns of its results, and then initiates the meal in which he symbolically offers body and blood and makes verbally clear that it is "for many" (14:24). We suggest that the placement of this meal and its additional meaning is Jesus' answer, in teaching and in action, to the question for deliberation that each disciple needs to ask: what should I do when faced with the temptation to betray? The answer: do not betray but stay faithful enough to participate in the cosmic order (14:25).

When we read the completed patterns of questioning in Mark, we see the situations early in the gospel resolved by action, climaxing in two incidents in the middle of the gospel in which real transformation occurs: the father of the sick child and the healing of Bartimaeus. As Jesus nears Jerusalem the narrative then shifts more to instruction of the cosmic order and how the divine *dynamis* may be accessed, and much less to demonstration. In other words, now in the narrative Jesus mostly teaches rather than performs miracles. But the fruit of his teaching, in the form of any transformation or appropriation of Jesus' message, is left unstated. We simply do not know for sure if any of the characters are able to separate from their previous erroneous judgments, endure the pain of liminality, and reach aggregation into the new vision of true healing and righteousness in God's cosmic order. For Mark's audience, perhaps the most optimistic passage for transformation is the Last Supper. There, in teaching and in action, Jesus makes transformation dramatically possible in the very ritual that the community for which Mark wrote continued to practice.

The Questioning Process Corrected by Jesus

One of the most interesting characteristics of Mark's gospel is the way the evangelist often shows Jesus correcting the questions of interlocutors. Jesus not only answers in an unexpected way questions that imply preconceived judgments; he also redirects those questions in light of the divine power being manifest in his actions and teaching. The result of his redirection is that their questioning now has the potential to produce fruit. Both of these trajectories—Jesus correcting questions and redirecting them—are shown in a series of three encounters in Mark 2:16–28. In the first, the scribes ask "Why does he eat with tax collectors and sinners?" Jesus' quick answer seems designed to unseat the previous judgment (it is wrong to eat with tax collectors and sinners). He then moves to answer a question for understanding, an essential question that his interlocutors should have asked but have neglected: who needs Jesus? "Those who are well have no need of a physician, but those who are sick; I have come to call not the righteous but sinners" (2:17).

In the next encounter people ask why Jesus' disciples do not fast as the Pharisees do and as John's disciples are doing, a direct challenge to Jesus as their teacher and therefore responsible for their behavior.[15] Again, the people seem to have made the previous judgment that fasting must be holier than not fasting. "The wedding guests cannot fast while the bridegroom is with them, can they?" (2:19). When the bridegroom is gone, their response will be fasting. In other words, Jesus with his parabolic response has rejected their assumption that fasting is not holy in and of itself. There is a time for rejoicing (when the divine *dynamis* is clearly perceived in the presence of Jesus, for example) and a time to fast.

---

15. Donahue, *Mark*, 106.

Having displayed two models for questions and answers in two pericopes, the series peaks with Jesus attempting to reorient the world view of the interlocutors in the question regarding the disciples picking grain on the Sabbath (2:23–28). Some Pharisees ask "Look, why are they doing what is not lawful on the Sabbath?" Again, the question is one for understanding, but a previous judgment provides the foundation for it: this action is always and in all circumstances wrong on the Sabbath. The assumption is mistaken: separation and movement into liminality and aggregation can never take place with that level of rigidity. Jesus reorients the questioning in a direction that anticipates a more expansive horizon than the questioners are currently displaying: "Have you not read what David did when he and his companions were hungry and in need of food?" The judgment is grounded in Scripture itself: in the case of hunger, it was right to eat the bread of the Presence, because humans are not the slaves of Sabbath laws, and the implied question for deliberation is: do you enslave yourselves and others to laws, or do you take laws into account while making prudential judgments in a specific situation? Even on a literal level, the answer is clear, but Jesus goes on: "the Son of Man is lord even of the Sabbath" (2:28). There we see the larger point of the entire series: this new experience of the divine *dynamis* calls for a reconsideration of previous judgments if one is to move into the process that leads to transformation in light of the now obvious cosmic order called "the kingdom of God."

We see in other ways in the Markan narrative that the questioning process does not necessarily move in one direction. During the storm on the sea (4:35–41), the disciples awaken Jesus and ask, "do you not care that we are perishing?" The question for judgment rather presumes the answer "no, you do not care." After rebuking the winds, Jesus shifts the question from judgment to understanding: "Why are you afraid?" The disciples, of course, know on the literal why they are afraid: the storm has put them in mortal danger. But they have not asked themselves the deeper question: what does it mean to have faith? Jesus then poses the challenge, "have you still no faith?"[16] That question should send them into a liminal space: given all the evidence they have seen and the separation from their previous lives that they have already experienced, is it not reasonable to be people of faith? The answer to the question for deliberation was already revealed in his stilling of the storm: they should believe and act appropriately, without such fear, aggregating themselves into the cosmic order Jesus reveals and brings about. But the pericope does not end there: in great awe, they ask, "Who then is this, that even the wind and the sea obey him?" The situation remains ambiguous. On the one hand, their "great awe" and their question show that on some level they are recognizing the divine presence, since their awe comes not as a result of the storm but of its calming.[17] On the other hand, the narrative leaves off without a direct answer to the question on the part of the disciples of Jesus' identity. It is clear to the reader, however, that Mark has provided more evidence of what he announced at the start of the gospel: that he is "Jesus Christ, the Son of God" (1:1).

A re-directed question for understanding can also lead to transformation, as is apparent in the pericope of the Gerasene demoniac (5:1–13). After Jesus has ordered the demon out of him, this man, like the earlier possessed man (1:21–28), initially asks what Jesus has to do with him. Jesus then reorients the question by asking the name of the demon. The answer he receives— Legion— is an obvious allusion to the Roman military and its domination. This allusion to the actual nature of the evil moves the process along. After the unclean spirits are driven into the swine and the swine driven into the sea, the healed man asks to go with Jesus: he recognizes and wants to be aggregated, to be part of this revelation of the true cosmic order, now legitimated by his own experience. His request followed by his personal transformation underline the sad fact that there are those who grasp Jesus' message but are

---

16. Moloney ("Mark 6:6–30," 662) puts it well: "This was the first explicit indication of the limitations of the fragile human beings called to be disciples of Jesus."

17. Dwyer, *Motif*, 111.

afraid to be part of it; they beg Jesus to leave their neighborhood. That Jesus gives the man more the role of witness rather than disciple does not reduce the drama of his transformation, taking up his role in the kingdom of God.

The healing of Jairus' daughter (5:35–43), framing the healing of the woman with hemorrhages, reveals more disordered questions to be corrected in a process that bears fruit for transformation. While Jesus is on his way with Jairus, who has seen enough to have reasonable belief that Jesus has the power to heal his daughter (5:23–24), the woman touches his cloak. She has already paid attention and has come to understand that Jesus' power is such that only a touch will heal her (5:25–28). Jesus' question about who touched him is a reasonable one given his experience of *dynamis* going out of his body, but it is followed by the disciples' literalist query, implying that his is a silly question to ask given the size of the crowd (5:30–31). The woman, in fear and trembling, falls before him, gestures in the Old Testament that indicate an appearance of the divine power. As Dwyer notes, "the motif of wonder here co-exists with belief, just as it co-existed with the crowd's praise of God after the healing of the paralytic in 2:12. This becomes especially important when it is noted that the woman functions in the gospel narrative as one of the "little people" whose faith constantly exemplifies the values of the reign of God and who serve as foils for the disciples."[18]

The question following the news of the death of Jairus' daughter, "Why trouble the teacher any further," as with the disciples' question in verse 31, implies a judgment that nothing can be done. Jesus redirects the issue, however, with his suggestive question of why they should weep when the girl is only sleeping (5:39). Their laughter shows their refusal to open themselves to new possibilities and experiences because of their rigid commitment to an inherited judgment that, while pragmatic enough, proves itself to be too narrow in the presence of the divine *dynamis* (5:35–39). Jesus' healing of the girl not only shows the error in their narrow horizon but also underlines the obvious answer to the question,

---

18. Ibid., 119.

"what should be done?" Jesus has already in verse 36 answered the implicit question for deliberation that they have to face: "Do not fear, only believe." Their being "overcome with amazement" points toward potential for transformation: they have seen the divine power and they know something new is afoot. Their reaction after this one event shows potential for transformed understanding; perhaps now they will be more like the woman who used to hemorrhage and is, through her reasonable faith in the presence of the divine *dynamis*, aggregative into God's cosmic order of life.

But there are times when, no matter how clearly Jesus tries to direct the process, the hoped-for transformation is not apparent in the narrative characters, though hope of course remains for the author's audience. In the first of two feeding miracles (6:30–42), Jesus tells the disciples to give the hungry people something to eat, implying that they should have seen enough by now to believe that something out of the ordinary could happen. Their response reveals their misunderstanding: they could not possibly have sufficient money for the amount of bread needed. Jesus reorients the process by asking "How many loaves have you?" then blesses and divides satisfactorily the fives loaves and two fish. The opportunity to welcome the revelation of God's reign and the obvious action required to participate in it is, however, lost at this point on the disciples. We learn this in the next scene: "Immediately he made his disciples get into the boat" (6:45) where they observe Jesus walking on the water, but "they were utterly astounded, for they did not understand about the loaves, but their hearts were hardened" (6:51–52). Since they did not understand that most basic lesson regarding the appearance of the divine *dynamis* and how to gain access to it, they could not understand another appearance when the wind ceased as Jesus entered the boat with them because of their fear. "Their fear and lack of understanding are interrelated. Their fear for their well-being prevents them from understanding, and their inability to understand leaves them frightened. Thus the issue is not a lack of intelligence. Mark is showing something more profound. Fear inhibits understanding, and misunderstanding generates fear. The disciples are vulnerable to both fear and a lack of understanding because the rule of God is both awesome and contrary to customary patterns of thinking."[19]

The disciples could not have been set up for success better than in the introduction Jesus gives them to the second feeding miracle Mark 8:1–10. He not only points out his own compassion for the crowd but underscores the people's desperate straits after three days without food and facing long journeys home. We should also note that this scene is Take Two of the disciples' opportunity to understand the significance of Jesus feeding the crowd. "How can one feed these people with bread here in the desert?" Their question was not the best way to pose their repeat misunderstanding, and it is hardly better than the previous "what, do you think money grows on trees?" judgment of 6:37. In fact, it might be considered worse because the first shows a practical concern whereas the second adds to it their religious failure to recognize in their own question a reflection of the Exodus manna in the desert (Exod 16:4–8). At this point the gospel's audience must now fear that the disciples suffer from chronic disbelief, and so Jesus again reframes the issue by changing the question: "How many loaves do you have?" That straightforward and practical question seeks and at least implicitly expects an answer.

The judgment that the people should be fed has already been made in Jesus' initial comments, and the action of the feeding itself answers the implicit question for deliberation: we must feed them. The continuing discourse about bread (8:14–21) shows no real progress toward transformation on the part of the disciples, and it leads to one of Jesus' most frustrated questions in Mark, to which he does not expect an answer but rather has already made the judgment for himself, a foreshadowing of the type of questions at end of the gospel: "Do you not yet understand?" (8:21). Even though they are with Jesus and see what is happening, they seem too frozen in their old commitments to "the way things are" to tolerate much time in liminal space.

Perhaps Mark depicts Jesus' most profound hope for the understanding and transformation of his closest followers and their

19. Rhoads et al., *Mark as Story*, 125.

apparent failure in two connected scenes about suffering (8:27–37 and 9:9–13) that surround the pivotal Transfiguration event. In the first scene, with the questions "Who do people say that I am?" and "Who do you say that I am?" (8:27–29), the potential hope is soon diminished. Peter's response ("you are the Messiah") provides a reasonable verbal answer, but by rejecting Jesus' teaching about his own suffering, Peter's grasp of the messianic title is exposed as a misunderstanding (8:32). He has inherited a traditional category within which he tries to place Jesus, but he cannot let go of his previous notion about what the coming messiah will actually do. Rather than attend to his own experience of Jesus, Peter attempts to fit Jesus into a familiar type. Jesus sharply rejects Peter's notion of the Messiah (8:33), then moves to indicate the necessary process of deliberation and action with both disciples and crowd: "If any want to become my followers, let them deny themselves and take up their cross and follow me" (8:34), a robust answer to the implied question for deliberation that Peter has just failed. Following the Transfiguration (9:9–13), the disciples question to themselves the matter of rising from the dead, then ask aloud, "why do the scribes say Elijah must come first?" This is one of the clearest indications that the disciples are held by the concepts of their previous mindset. Jesus tries to reorient the focus yet again on the sufferings to come with his alternative question for understanding, "How then is it written about the Son of Man, that he is to go through many sufferings and be treated with contempt?" The insertion "is it written" is a mocking of both scribes and disciples, highlighting his frustration with the process.

    The tension only builds and the difficulties increase as Jesus nears Jerusalem, as is shown in several pericopes in Mark 10:1–45. In three different scenes, Jesus asks the simplest questions for understanding, but each leads to a teaching that reveals the power of bias and the difficulty of being liberated from it. In the first (10:2–12), to the Pharisees' question for judgment about whether it is lawful for a man to divorces his wife, Jesus simply returns to a question for understanding: "What did Moses command you?" (10:3). They try to trap Jesus, and in return, Jesus traps them in a rigid, limited, and in this case androcentric horizon of literalism, then instructs them to the more challenging and life-giving vision of the kingdom of God that insists on the equality of female and male agents as depicted in Genesis. To the man's question for deliberation, "what must I do to inherit eternal life," Jesus returns with a question of his own, "why do you call me good? No one is good but God alone" (10:17–18). Just as with the Pharisees, Jesus simply but pointedly refocuses the exchange on the vision of God that he has attempted to demonstrate throughout the gospel. In the third, Jesus asks two questions of James and John: "What is it you want me to do for you?" and "are you able to drink the cup that I drink, or be baptized with the baptism that I am baptized with?" (10:36, 38). In each case, Jesus focuses on the challenge of transformation, of letting go of preconceived notions and even preconceived questions, to attend to what God brings by expanding the horizons of the believer (10:11, 21, 39). By receiving and trusting and acting with the poverty and openness of those lowest in the society (10:15, 23, 43–44) one is able to leave behind the privilege and its biased, egocentric construction of reality in favor of a painful yet fruitful liminal process. There is no other way to reasonable belief and aggregation into God's reality. The point is underscored by the response of faith, discussed above, in the scene of Bartimaeus' healing and resulting discipleship.

The final two questions for reorientation reveal continuing resistance in some who encounter Jesus. The first, "is it lawful to pay taxes to the emperor, or not?" (12:14), is asked by some Pharisees and Herodians in order to trap him. As he approaches his execution, the entire situation shows what Jesus is up against with regard to some in the religious establishment, who function as a local extension of the powers of Rome. Jesus' response is the real question: "Why are you putting me to the test?" but he follows with a question that turns the tables on them: "Whose head is this, and whose title?" (12:16). Their answer is ostensibly one of simple fact (it is indeed the emperor's representation) but also leaves them in danger of revealing their own bias in their actions: do they believe that anything is owed to the empire, or is everything owed to God? (12: 17).

The second of the two final questions also expresses a lack of understanding and serves to heighten the reader's anticipation of doom. "Why was this ointment wasted in this way?" when it could have been sold and the money used to aid the poor (14:4–5). Jesus' response suggests that the disciples need to realize the right question to ask. "Let her alone, why do you trouble her?" Since Jesus affirms that "she has done what she could" (14:6, 8), the implication is that the disciples have not done what they could. Jesus identifies the ointment with his burial, and so the disciples have failed to get the point of his impending death. Their failure is accentuated when one considers that Mark begins his gospel by setting Jesus' face toward his execution: "Now after John was arrested, Jesus came to Galilee, proclaiming the good news of God" (Mark 1:14).

As the narrative shows Jesus reorienting questions, sometimes the characters follow his lead and turn to the vision of the kingdom of God, but more often they show various types of rigid bias, inherited judgments and a resulting unwillingness to take the next step, whether that is one of separation or liminality or aggregation. In Mark, even Jesus' self-sacrifice on the cross does not guarantee the immediate transformation of the disciples.

The Questioning Process Frustrated

Mark sprinkles his narrative with painful examples of a questioning process that could result in transformation but does not; these examples are usually indicated by a rhetorical question of Jesus that falls on the deaf ears of people who are so recalcitrant that the narrative leaves no hope that they will get the point. Early in the gospel, for example, there is the scene of the man with the withered hand in the synagogue (3:1–6). After a series of challenges initiated by the Herodians and others, Jesus seizes this opportunity at the synagogue to ask for the first time in gospel, "Is it lawful to good or to do harm on the Sabbath, to save life or to kill?" In this situation, Jesus does not even bother with a question for understanding; in fact, the question that he does ask is so absurd as to be considered rhetorical, but with a clear purpose: to help the skeptical crowd to see the absurdity of their recalcitrance. Their silence and their refusal even to consider the meaning of Jesus' healing warrant Jesus' anger and grief. Although Jesus restores the man's hand, the point of the pericope is that the recalcitrance of some of the Pharisees and Herodians intensifies and they conspire to kill Jesus. Their very attention to the events happening in front of them is so inadequate that they refuse to ask even enough of a question about these events to begin to separate from their previous mindset.

Soon it is the disciples who fall under the rhetorical sword of Jesus' frustration. Again he omits any help for their understanding, as if he knows they are not ready even to enter the process. "Do you not understand this parable? Then how will you understand all the parables?" (4:13). While he does explain the parable to them, his most serious advice comes in the simple phrase "pay attention" (4:24). There is no hope of insight without attention to experience, whether the experience comes in hearing a teaching or observing an action. A comparable level of frustration in 7:17–19 over what can defile a person (after a lengthy explanation by Jesus) offers at this point no indication of insight on the part of the disciples.

A series of questions in Mark 6:1–6, ending without genuine reflection, highlights the problem of previous bias that allows no room for insight into experience. Here, the result of Jesus teaching in the synagogue, are a series of questions that initially seem to make a good start toward understanding: "Where did this man get all this? What is this wisdom that has been given to him?" and they recognize that "deeds of power" are indeed being performed by him. But immediately, without reflection, the questioners then jump ahead to a rhetorical question that reveals that their bias is still in place: "Is this not the carpenter, the son of Mary and brother of James and Joses and Judas and Simon, and are not his sisters here with us?" Their experience of Jesus' goodness and wisdom cannot be real because of his family connections. Their judgment stems from his human provenance rather than from their attention to and understanding of his deeds, and so they take offence at him. Rather than separate themselves from their previous attitudes, they remain enslaved to their bias, seeking "to integrate the problematic sector into what is already unproblematic,"[20] and the result is gloomy: few deeds of power could be done there, "and he [Jesus] was amazed at their unbelief."

The pericope that shows the opposite result of Jesus' encounter with Bartimaeus is not the earlier healing of the anonymous blind man, although that story helps to dramatize Bartimaeus' transformation. It is rather the exchange between Jesus and the chief priests, scribes and elders as Jesus and the disciples return to Jerusalem (11:27–33). When they ask by what authority Jesus acts, he responds with a question of his own that seeks a reversal of their misunderstanding: whether John's baptism was from heaven or of human origin. In fact, the question is a rhetorical one that exposes their concern not to seek the truth but to be right in the eyes of those in the Temple, the place of authority. "Underlying their dilemma is the even more basic question: Which is more important—the kingdom of God proclaimed by John and Jesus or the Jerusalem Temple (whose guardians were the chief priests, scribes, and elders)?"[21] Their egoism prevents them from being able to make a judgment about John's baptism, and the progress that could be gained from reasonable reflection is completely stymied.

The section of the Gospel from Gethsemane to the end is replete with a list of what we can only call rhetorical questions and exercises in futility. Jesus' interlocutors either do not seek real understanding or they so misunderstand the situation that even when a genuine question is posed, it goes nowhere. When Jesus returns from prayer, his question about his three disciples sleeping is not a question for understanding but one of frustration, not expecting an answer (14:32–42) any more than he does in the scene of his arrest (14:43–50). The questions of the high priest (14:60–65) and Pilate (15:1–15) seek only a condemnation that will give them excuses to justify their actions. Whether in the

---

20. Berger and Luckman, *Social Construction*, 24.
21. Donahue, *Mark*, 335.

frustrated questions put forward by Jesus or the machinations of his accusers, true understanding is not on the horizon and hope of transformation is absent.

The Markan Jesus, master of inquiry, asks his own desperate question for understanding at the scene of his crucifixion: "Why have you forsaken me?" (15:34), "one of the seismic epicenters of the Christian Bible where the great tectonic plates of the reign of God collide with the anguish of human suffering and the experience of Godforsakenness."[22] It is both a question for understanding and an encouragement for the authorial audience to imitate Jesus' example of faithfulness. Whether ancient or modern, all must ask the same question, sometimes when suffering innocently as Jesus did, at other times as a question directed to a mirror: "Whom am I forsaking, and why? What am I doing to myself and to others?" That the question is a quotation from Psalm 22 means that for the attentive auditor, it holds within in the seeds for adequate judgment and deliberation: trust that God's good resolution of this obvious evil is within sight.

Interestingly, the final question of the gospel epitomizes the general lack of insight shown by Jesus' opponents and many of his followers in the narrative: "Who will roll away the stone for us from the entrance to the tomb?" (16:3). They haven't the slightest expectation of what they will immediately find (or not find, as the case may be). As is typical of Mark, the ending of the scene is ambiguous and the actual answer is to be provided by the gospel's audience. The author's intended frustration in much of the narrative continues to the end as that the disciples still aren't asking the intelligent question; and now Jesus isn't there to correct the process immediately. The only indication of hope is the possibility that rolling back the stone will prompt in the disciples the insight that the cosmic order revealed by Jesus is real, and in fact, the authorial audience knows it is real, because they know that the women did tell, and that Peter and the others after the resurrection answered fruitfully the questions for understanding, reflection, and deliberation. These first witnesses, this audience knows, were

22. Jinkins and Reid, "God's Forsakenness," 33.

indeed fully aggregated and went on to proclaim the reign of God as they continued to experience it in and with the risen Jesus. So in fact, the question for deliberation is most poignantly addressed by means of the open ending to the audience. As Yung Suk Kim describes it, "The last scene of the Gospel of Mark is open-ended. Mark's readers are invited to ask and answer the question What could they do? The Markan community can grow and continue its faith . . . But this is not a linear process; it is circular."[23] Despite fits and starts, moving forward only to step again backward, the process of understanding, reflection, and deliberation is the human process of self-transcendence that continues toward the covenanted liberation from various types of bondage that the Markan Jesus intends.[24]

Conclusion

Commentators have noted the comparative lack of ethical injunctions in this gospel, attributing it to various causes such as its purported gnostic tendencies, eschatology, or focus on Christology.[25] We suggest that Telford is on the right track when he opens up the issue in Mark of "spirituality" and "interiority"[26] in a sense more agreeable with our modern concerns than this first-century work is often given credit for.

We see in the Gospel of Mark the self-disposing love of Jesus as the answer to questions for deliberation: what are we to do? The healings and acts of "power" are not just to display the divine *dynamis* but to help those present and those who come after to prepare their minds to accept it, to believe *enough* to enter the process of separation from previous judgments, the painful liminal period, and the aggregation into the cosmic order of God that Jesus reveals in actions and in words. The divisions of the questioning process

---

23. Kim, *Transformative*, 44.
24. Dowd and Malbon, "Significance," 297.
25. Telford, *Theology*, 221.
26. Ibid., 221–22.

used above are not intended as a rigid taxonomy but as an indication of how many ways there are into this process that leads to transformation, at how many points the signposts can be reasonably followed or stubbornly denied.

Questioning is the dynamic process that can lead to self-transcendence. Some stories in Mark's gospel show this process leading to self-transcendence in its narrative characters. Other stories reveal the blind spots, biases and rigid assumptions that discourage or block the enlightenment that Jesus' words and deeds are intended to deliver. The restricted questions posed by those who are unwilling to change, as well as the frustrated rhetorical questions expressed by Jesus, uncover the painful struggle for an expansive horizon that is able to hope for and work toward the new vision of the cosmic order that Jesus calls the kingdom of God.

3
The Gospel of John

We have been examining the role of questions in the process of human transformation. When carried out authentically, that process leads to a reasonable faith in the experience of the divine *dynamis*, which in turn promotes the transformation. This transformation that we have called self-transcendence can only go forward, however, if there is a willingness to enter a process that entails separation, liminality, and aggregation. In other words, beyond the experience of the divine presence there must be reflection on it, and only then can one be reborn as a disciple. The refusal of self-transcendence by clinging to previous judgments that experience now reveals to be inadequate blocks the necessary growth in the way of God that Jesus presents and embodies.

The gospels of Mark and John are not always thought of together, but on the issue of the characters' understanding the divine *dynamis* through a process of questioning, they indeed pair together nicely. The role of questions leading to understanding has been more clearly recognized in John, due to their many occurrences in extended scenes that press the audiences toward a less literal and more spiritual understanding of reality and thus toward transformation.

Let us recall a point made in the first chapter: understanding is the grasp of the intelligibility in the data of experience; when understanding is ignored and concepts are imposed on the data, then what is new in experience cannot be grasped. In other words, a judgment unexamined in the light of new experience may very well impede new insights. The extended encounters narrated in the Fourth Gospel demonstrate that rigidly maintained previous judgments can support a view of the world limited to literal interpretation without room for the spiritual. In spite of new experiential evidence, some characters display a refusal to risk liminality, even if they have tip-toed into separation. But the extended encounters in John's gospel show more than that: as in the Gospel of Mark, some characters do express an openness to liminality and aggregation, to authentic belief and genuine transformation. The gospel narrates both successes and failures of self-transcendence.

Beginning as Conclusion

The prologue (1:1–18) of John has been compared successfully to an overture, pointing toward the themes that will be developed throughout the gospel.[1] One of those themes is the contrast, especially developed in Israelite Wisdom literature, between those who did not accept the presence of God (Wisdom, Logos) as "true light" entering the world and those who "received" and "believed" (1:9–13). These verses introduce us to varied vocabulary for the process of understanding that will reappear throughout the gospel. This true light in our narrative is the fully incarnate Logos (1:14). This dichotomy, between those who accept the true light and those who do not, guides the presentations of encounters in the narrative as fully as it does the revelation of Lady Wisdom and her acceptance/rejection in the book of Proverbs and other Wisdom literature. The author of the Fourth Gospel here however, concurs with and presents aspects of Wisdom as traditional,[2] and like the Israelite sages he allows, indeed insists upon, engagement with the process of gaining wisdom. In other words, the Gospel of John develops wisdom motifs by dramatizing the characters' coming

---

1. Heitmüller, *Johannes-Evangelium*, 37.
2. Talbert, *Reading John*, 68–69.

to reasonable belief when their experience of Jesus requires them to ask new questions about tradition. Here the conclusion of the evangelist/sage is clearly presented in the beginning: "And the Word became flesh and lived among us, and we have seen his glory" (1:14). When characters in the Fourth Gospel make correct judgments, they have understood that they are experiencing the presence of this Word. Most of the important questions in John revolve around two closely related issues: where is Jesus from and who is he? The characters need to go beyond the literal (e.g. where Jesus is literally *from*) in order to grasp *who* Jesus is. Throughout the gospel we will see characters both fail and succeed in grasping the spiritual insight that transcends the literal level of the encounter and opens onto self-transcendence.

Even though the prologue does not include all of the characters' routes that the narrative will explore, we do have snapshots of these paths if we consider the "beginning" of the gospel more broadly than the prologue, through John 2. Those routes continue to be presented in the form of questions and answers through these chapters, which present brief types of authentic and of inauthentic or fruitless processes of questioning that will be expanded later in the narrative. It is no accident that the first question comes quickly after the conclusions of the prologue, when emissaries from "the Jews"[3] come to ask John the Baptist a seemingly genuine ques-

---

3. Given the history of Christian oppression of Jews, the imprecise moniker "the Jews" employed for only some people, and often with hostility, in the Fourth Gospel is extremely problematic. While exactly to which historical group (if any) the author is referring remains under debate, for our purposes in this study we note that the term characterizes those who rarely are able to break out of their literalism or their previous judgments to incorporate the evidence of Jesus they are experiencing. For a competent and brief summary of the general issue, see, for example, Keener, *Gospel of John*, 214–28. For a recent treatment that highlights well the literary complexities, see Zimmerman, "The Jews," 71–109. We maintain the quotation marks around the phrase to remind us that this phrase refers only to those people in the narrative most strongly resisting new experience of the divine in Jesus. That resistance in this vein is a human problem not distinct to any particular religion can be seen in the recent words of Pope Francis (Spadaro, "Heart"): "If the Christian is a restorationist, a legalist, if he wants everything clear and safe, then he will find nothing. Tradition and memory of the past must help us to have the courage to open up new

tion for understanding: "Who are you?" (1:19). As Moloney says, that question "could be taken as the *leitmotif* of the Fourth Gospel. Response to that question will determine the success of failure of all who encounter the Johannine Jesus."[4] The questioners begin to mine their traditional trove of potential answers, a perfectly reasonable procedure: are you Elijah, the prophet, or who? John gives them an answer that they cannot immediately fit into one of their inherited categories, even though John's quotation from Isaiah (1:23) is a completely legitimate, if enigmatic, answer from the tradition. The questioners immediately conclude that if he does not fit into one of the categories they expected to hear, he should not be baptizing (1:24). John, however, answers by correcting their concern; the real question is, whom is John announcing? John is essentially correcting their hasty judgment by showing them what they have failed to attend to in his quotation from Isaiah: "Make straight the way of the Lord." The failure to pay attention is one of the roots of misunderstanding.

John the Baptist presents evidence for his judgments concerning Jesus (such as his claim that Jesus is the Lamb of God) when he recounts his experience of Jesus' baptism (1:32–34). John's judgment, expressed in a phrase that echoes and expands traditional sacrificial lamb imagery, is enticing enough to two of his disciples that they follow Jesus, only to be questioned by him: "What are you looking for?" (1:38). Their response is yet another question: "where are you staying?" (1:38). The disciples are seeking genuine knowledge of Jesus and use the same term used by John the Baptist in his description of the Holy Spirit at the baptism: The Spirit was "staying" with Jesus and the disciples want to know where Jesus is "staying" (*menō*). The question about where Jesus is literally staying signals the deeper spiritual concern: how does one abide or remain with Jesus? When Andrew announces to his brother, "We

---

areas to God. Those who today always look for disciplinarian solutions, those who long for an exaggerated doctrinal 'security,' those who stubbornly try to recover a past that no longer exists—they have a static and inward-directed view of things. In this way, faith becomes an ideology among other ideologies."

4. Moloney, *Gospel of John*, 58.

have found the Messiah" (1:41), it is not precisely clear what he means by that title, but his claim is a start toward understanding. One step at a time.

In contradistinction to the initial set of questions from the priests and Levites that ends in fruitlessness, the next section in the Gospel shows the questioning process turning in the other direction. Denying the judgment of Philip that he had found the Messiah, based on his evaluation of a brief experience of Jesus, Nathaniel jumps to judgment: "Can anything good come out of Nazareth?" (1:46). The focus on Jesus' place of origin is a restriction to the literal that will time and again prove a barrier to understanding who Jesus is. Nathaniel's false start reveals a prior and irrelevant judgment, but it is not fatal for the process of questioning that the gospel dramatizes. Philip simply responds with a reference to the evidence: "Come and see" (1:46). The verb "see" introduces another bit of vocabulary indicating understanding that will reappear throughout the gospel: to "believe" and to "know" are almost synonymous[5] and to "see" can serve as a metaphor for them, even though it is possible to see a sign and still not believe or know (12:36–37). Nathanael responds to Jesus' seemingly prophetic knowledge this time with a question for understanding rather than an imposition of inherited prejudice. He is satisfied with Jesus' response, and declares him to be Son of God and King of Israel (1:49). The fact that he may not fully understand what he has said, as Jesus hints (1:50), does not change the fact that an openness to new experience and a re-evaluation of past judgments is the door to deliberation and transformation.[6]

---

5. Moloney, *Gospel of John*, 232; Brown, *Gospel according to John*, 1:298.

6. Keener (*Gospel of John*, 475) suggests that Andrew's announcement "may reflect his interpretation of John's testimony about the lamb (1:29) interpreted through the grid of his own experience of Jesus. In the same way, Philip's testimony about Jesus messiahship provides the categories for Nathanael to interpret Jesus' supernatural knowledge (1:45, 49). In John's theology, both the christological witness of disciples and the personal experience of Christ become necessary for adequate faith."

Captivity to a literalist interpretation of Jesus' origins is depicted in the Temple pericope (2:13–22)[7] when "the Jews" ask "what sign can you show us for doing this?" Jesus' response is, "destroy this temple and in three days I will raise it up." Their resulting question displays a failure we will see repeatedly in the gospel: "This temple has been under construction for forty-six years, and will you raise it up in three days?" Later in the gospel the narrator tells us that the disciples recalled Jesus' prediction, and this memory contributes to their own belief in his resurrection. That passage not only underscores to the authorial audience that the disciples will find the path to understanding but the recollection also demonstrates the important truth that understanding sometimes comes gradually. "We readers, however, in the light of our knowledge of the total story are invited to grasp those implications right here at this early stage of the narrative. We are being taught to read between the lines of the story, to grasp from the start the nonliteral, symbolic meaning, and to have our faith deepened by seeing now what the disciples saw only at the end: how Jesus' action, symbolically understood, foreshadows the contest that will climax at his 'hour' (cf. 2:4), fulfilling a script laid down in the scripture."[8]

In the initial section of the gospel, therefore, are clear statements of the goal: that the audience (whether narrative or authorial) might engage traditional knowledge, which is then expanded by experience, to come to authentic judgments. We have also seen snapshots of the different ways that the process can develop and conclude. The process of questioning, which is crucial in this transformation, can begin well and end in fruitlessness, or it can begin well and end in life-changing insight. Finally, it can begin poorly and end with progress toward transformation, as we shall see below. The key to a successful outcome is a willingness to

---

7. Jesus' response to his mother at Cana, literally "what have you to do with me" (2:4) we read not as a genuine question but as a (temporary, it turns out) refusal to be involved. See Giblin, "Suggestion," 197–211.

8. Byrne, *Life Abounding*, 62.

reevaluate traditional categories based on the reasonable evidence of new experience.

From Snapshots to Vignettes

Through chapter 5, we see these snapshots expanded into what we might think of as short dramatic scenes depicting the same options. Representing the barrier of literalness, we have Nicodemus, who approaches Jesus with a judgment already formed: "no one can do these signs that you do apart from the presence of God" (3:2). It's not the worst start. Nicodemus understands of Jesus, either through his own, immanently generated knowledge or by believing someone else's reasonable testimony, and he has concluded that these are indeed signs of God's presence. His judgment in the form of the title "teacher," however, is certainly quite limited in comparison to what others like John the Baptist have already concluded. His growth would have been more promising had it started with a question for understanding rather than a reaffirmation of a traditional judgment, because as soon as Jesus presses him to a deeper understanding, he hits a wall with the double meanings of "born again" and "spirit" (3:3–9). Jesus then meets Nicodemus' opening judgment with one of his own: "Are you a teacher of Israel, and yet you do not understand these things?" (3:10) and goes on to explain that Nicodemus is trapped in the "earthly" or literal and hence cannot "believe" (3:11–21).

When Jesus encounters a sick man by the Sheep Gate, he asks perhaps the most spiritually profound question in the entire gospel: "Do you want to be made well?" (5:6). The sick man's non-answer "pity party" list of excuses (5:7) does not bode well for the questioning process, showing as it does that he is trapped by prior judgments about his condition. To say that the man was "made well" (5:9) is ironic because it is only physical wellness, shown in the following scene in which he finds out Jesus' name through another encounter and reports back to those who seek to persecute Jesus, apparently cooperating with them. Like the first blind man in Mark, one does not want to minimize the physical healing, but it is not necessarily identical with or even a sign of spiritual and moral transformation.

Significantly, it is at the end of a long discourse connected to the sign of healing on the Sabbath (5:1–47) that Jesus asks rhetorical questions that leave little hope for understanding among those opposed to the healing and to his supposedly blasphemous claims. Jesus essentially accuses the accusers of claiming to know all about the witness of Scripture, especially Moses, yet not recognizing that same power of God in Jesus' actions and identity: "How can you believe when you accept glory from one another and do not seek the glory that comes from the one who alone is God? . . . If you believed Moses, you would believe me, for he wrote about me. But if you do not believe what he wrote how will you believe what I say?" (5:44, 46–47). Their system is a closed one in which they congratulate each other for their firm convictions that leave no room for experiencing what they claim to believe. Their defect foreshadows a longer episode later in the gospel with ultimately the same result: the questioners ultimately prefer human glory to the glory of God (12:42–43).

From the beginning of the gospel to this point, we see the various shapes that the questions for understanding (seeing, belief, accepting, receiving, knowing) can take both positively and negatively. Small steps forward can be gained with some persistence on all sides of the encounter, as in the case of Nathanael. But when Jesus' interlocutors cling to narrow prejudgments and only the most literal meanings of words, they erect significant barriers to understanding more deeply where Jesus is from and consequently who he is. The next chapters (6–11) will develop these options into extended, multifaceted scenes that explore all possible outcomes in more depth and detail.

The Longer Discourses

One of the most enlightening and delightful aspects of this gospel is the author's skill at weaving various approaches of characters and their consequent levels of success into coherent scenes that contain multiple encounters. One of these scenes comes early in the encounter with the Samaritan Woman. We see a much more promising beginning than that of Nicodemus with her question, "How is it that you, a Jew, ask a drink of me, a woman of Samaria?" (4:9). Prompted by an implied value judgment that they have both inherited, i.e. Jesus should not be doing this, she raises the question why then is he doing it? The answer to this question for understanding will ultimately challenge the received value judgment. Jesus suggests that if she knew a little more she would have had a much better question. He sidesteps, in other words, her literal identification of him as "a Jew" and, perhaps sensing the openness of an inquisitive and intelligent person (which certainly the evangelist hopes the audience is), moves directly into the symbolism of "living water." The woman responds with two more questions: "Where do you get that living water? Are you greater than our ancestor Jacob . . . ?" (4:11–12). The first question, for understanding, shows that Jesus has destabilized her inherited judgment. The second is perhaps rhetorical, implying disbelief, but it may also reveal a desire for deeper understanding. These questions, limited but apparently sincere, open up a dialogue that leads the woman to know that Jesus is at least a prophet and even to question whether he could be the Messiah (4:16–30). "Also remarkable is the fact that it is while she is still asking questions, still wondering about the status of Jesus . . . that the woman begins to attract people to Jesus. Her journey of faith is far from complete. Yet already, as her townsfolk come out from the city and approach him, it is having an apostolic effect (v. 30). True conversion of heart necessarily draws in others as well, and a faith still asking many questions is no less effective to that end."[9] Her knowledge is limited but it prompts an implied question for deliberation (unlike those of Nicodemus): what should I do with this knowledge? Her answer is to share it (4:28–29), bringing other Samaritan townspeople into the encounter and thus into the quest for understanding, judgment, and deliberation concerning Jesus (4:39–42).

9. Byrne, *Life Abounding*, 87–88.

As we have come to expect, the layered and complex interactions recounted in John 6 are spurred by the questioning process. In the actual feeding scene (6:1–14), Jesus himself uses it as a tactic (according to the narrator), by asking Philip regarding the crowd: "Where are we to buy bread for these people to eat?" Philip's dismissive comment is a judgment regarding a purely practical matter that does not transcend the literal level: "Six months' wages would not buy enough bread for each of them to get a little." Andrew, only slightly more hopefully, suggests the boy's five loaves and two fish, but then asks the important question: "what are they among so many people?" That is in fact the correct question for understanding, as Jesus reveals when he feeds the crowd, acting out answers both to an implicit question for judgment (it is enough) and for deliberation (feed them!).

The complex scene continues when the people find Jesus (6:22–40), who had set out to escape their ambitions for him, and ask, "Rabbi, when did you come here?" Jesus answers a different question, one that would have been more relevant: "why are we following him?" In doing so, he encourages them to work for the "food of eternal life." They indeed follow his lead and shift to a better question: "What must we do to perform the works of God?" (6:28). When Jesus tells them they must believe in the one God has sent, they draw on tradition as they search for understanding: "What sign are you going to give us then, so that we may see it and believe you? What work are you performing? Our ancestors ate the manna in the wilderness; as it is written, 'He gave them bread from heaven to eat.'" In answering their question Jesus corrects their exegesis: "Very truly, I tell you, it was not Moses who gave you the bread from heaven, but it is my Father who gives you the true bread from heaven. For the bread of God is that which comes down from heaven and gives life to the world." (6:32). Like a genuine seeker (e.g., the Samaritan woman) they continue to follow his lead, making progress without yet fully comprehending: "Sir, give us this bread always" (6:33).

But as so often happens, previous judgments and literal thinking block correct understanding. "The Jews" begin to complain about his identification of himself with the bread from heaven:[10] "Is not this Jesus, the son of Joseph, whose father and mother we know? How can he now say, 'I have come down from heaven'?" (6:42). Every hint that Jesus tries to give about his origin with the Father that would help them understand the image of his flesh for the life of the world only compounds their confusion and highlights their lack of spiritual insight. "How can this man give us his flesh to eat?" Even the disciples ask "who can accept" the teaching about eating the flesh and drinking the blood of the Son of Man.

Finally, after more probing to help move them toward understanding, Jesus asks a question for reflection: "Do you also wish to go away?" and Peter is able to make a reasonable judgment: "We have come to believe and know that you are the Holy One of God" (6:67–69). "For the first time in the narrative a character has expressed faith in Jesus for the right reason: *his origins*."[11] The crowd and the disciples stick with it and make progress, while those who hold on to narrow interpretations of previous judgments do not.

In John 7, Jesus himself focuses explicitly on the importance of right judgment, a focus that seems only to lead the interlocutors to rush to the opposite judgment. "Do not judge by appearances, but judge with right judgement" (7:24). Those judging by appearances rather than experience again focus on where the messiah is supposed to come from. Again the crowd represents division about Jesus, while "the Jews" represent those who almost always refuse to budge in their understanding (7:10–23, 31, 40–44). As soon as Jesus counsels all not to judge "by appearances, but judge with right judgment," some in the narrative audience go down the wrong path: "Yet we know where this man is from; but when the Messiah comes, no one will know where he is from" (7:24, 27).

The Pharisees compound the problem with their literalism after Jesus says that he will soon go to the one who sent him: "Does he intend to go to the Dispersion among the Greeks and teach the

---

10. As Keener (*Gospel of John*, 685) points out, the language hearkens back to the wilderness murmuring (Exod 16:2 etc.), but here they grumble *after* receiving bread, underscoring their negative attitude.

11. Moloney, *Gospel of John*, 229.

Greeks?" (7:35), and in this pericope, the literalism that imprisons their understanding has the final word. When the police who were to arrest Jesus instead return empty-handed and apparently impressed by Jesus, the questions of the Pharisees continue to betray their obstinacy: "'Why did you not arrest him?' The police answered, 'Never has anyone spoken like this!' Then the Pharisees replied, 'Surely you have not been deceived too, have you? Has any one of the authorities or of the Pharisees believed in him?" (7:45–48). As Byrne points out, "The irony is that the common people (including the police) are at least asking questions about Jesus, while the authorities by contrast, for all their knowledge of the law, are held back by malevolence from any inclination to give Jesus a hearing and possibly move toward faith."[12] Even when facing the tentative suggestion by Nicodemus that Jesus be given a hearing the Pharisees insist, "Surely you are not also from Galilee, are you? Search and you will see that no prophet is to arise from Galilee" (7:52).

The resistance to understanding the spiritual meaning of location (where Jesus is from, where he is going) continues in John 8:12–59, showing the interlocutors, despite one brief moment of hope, spiraling away from the process that leads toward aggregation in God's order.[13] Their questions "where is your Father?" and "is he going to kill himself" seem initially to stymie them in continued confusion (8:19, 27). And yet, the narrative takes a surprising turn: "As he was saying these things, many believed in him" (8:30).

Immediately, however, the alert auditor hears a clue that this belief will ultimately not be enough to bear fruit: "Then Jesus said to the Jews who had believed in him, 'If you continued in my word, you are truly my disciples; and you will know the truth, and the truth will make you free'" (8:31–32). The significant verb *menō* (here translated "continue") appears here. If they choose to "abide" or "continue" with Jesus, they would risk having to leave

---

12. Byrne, *Life Abounding*, 141.

13. Presuming that John 8:1–11 is a later addition, 8:12–59 is continuing at least thematically the scene in John 7.

the standard, received interpretation of the tradition in favor of God's renewed order that Jesus brings and embodies. This liminal process would release them from their bondage to a literal meaning of the tradition, signified in their excessive pride as sons of Abraham. "They answered him, 'We are descendants of Abraham and have never been slaves to anyone. What do you mean by saying, "You will be made free"?'" (8:33). They can technically say that they themselves have not been physically enslaved, and they can assert that they have always been spiritually free,[14] yet the shallowness of the answer is spiritually bankrupt. Moreover, there was literal slavery of the people in Egypt, in Babylon and virtual slavery under the Romans. "We have never been slaves" is only the narrowest, most literal truth.

When Jesus says, "I declare what I have seen in the Father's presence; as for you, you should do what you have heard from the Father" (8:39), he admits that they *hear*, that is, in a sense they understand and have come to believe, but now it's time for a question for deliberation: what shall they *do*? Here is where they fail the process due to their refusal to release their excessive pride in being sons of Abraham, refusing to say that Abraham also would behave differently. They are conceiving Abraham in the image of their own failures (8:39–41). In the end, even though they hear, their failure adds up to the same as not believing at all (8:45–47, 52). Throughout, their spiritual bondage is expressed by focusing on their literal descent from Abraham and their literal creation by God; they cannot move to what it means to be a spiritual follower of Abraham or of God. Ironically, their dilemma here, and its sad resolution, foreshadows that of Pontius Pilate.

Just when the situation seems desperate indeed for the characters in the gospel, we have the masterful pericope of the man born blind (9:1–41). It begins with a culturally expected question from the disciples: "Rabbi, who sinned, this man or his parents, that he was born blind?"[15] After assuring them that the handicap does not

---

14. Carson, *Gospel according to John*, 349.

15. Such beliefs were widespread enough that in Berger's terms we would call them "objectivations" (Berger and Luckman, *Social Construction*, 60–61).

result from sin, Jesus heals the man and thus demonstrates one of the primary images of the prologue: that Jesus is the light of the world. The Pharisees are divided: some have concluded, based on a prior judgment, that anyone who does not keep Sabbath as they understand it cannot be representing the divine *dynamis*. Others, however, are trying to understand, given the experience of a man healed: "How can a man who is a sinner perform such signs?" (9:16). When the blind man is asked what he has to say, he is able to step out bravely and answer the key question, who is Jesus: "He is a prophet."

As the focus shifts to the parents of the man born blind, the description of the interlocutors also shifts from "Pharisees" (who were divided) to "Jews," the gospel's perhaps slightly more pointed language for those trapped in literalism and/or previous judgments that present experience shows are limited or erroneous. Here, these particular Jews refuse even to acknowledge that the experience even happened, denying that he had been blind and had been healed, hence the involvement of the parents who fear the authorities (9:17–22). The fear of the parents is understandable in the context: "they are characters who give *witness* to the dangers of confessing Jesus, the explicit motivation for their claim to limited knowledge," and their fear also serves to highlight the bravery of their son.[16] The healed man will not be trapped in their small horizon and sticks to the reality of the experience, even though he is in the liminal state of not yet knowing how exactly to interpret it: "I do not know whether he is a sinner. One thing I do know, that though I was blind, now I see." Pressed by more of their inane questions, the man strikes back: "I have told you already, and you would not listen. Why do you want to hear it again? Do you also want to become his disciples?" (9:27). The deeply hopeful aspect for all human questioning is represented in the rapid progress of the man born blind, in spite of the opposition he faced; the rigid

---

For a review of various aspects of that belief in the ancient Mediterranean, see Keener, *Gospel of John*, 777–79.

16. Labahn, "Parents," 449–50.

focus of the questioners on knowing where Jesus comes from is obviously absurd in the face of the blind man's experience:

> Here is an astonishing thing! You do not know where he comes from, and yet he opened my eyes. We know that God does not listen to sinners, but he does listen to one who worships him and obeys his will. Never since the world began has it been heard that anyone opened the eyes of a person born blind. If this man were not from God, he could do nothing. (9:31–33)

The opposition's denial of the blind man's own experience presses him to keep thinking, drawing on the aspects of his religious tradition most relevant to what he has just experienced, and he arrives at an authentic understanding of Jesus: where is this man from? From God. His new understanding of the cosmic order embodied in Jesus' actions is taking shape.

Finding the man he had healed, Jesus presses him to further judgment: "Do you believe in the Son of Man?" The assurance from Jesus draws upon two familiar gospel terms for understanding, seeing and hearing: "You have seen him, and the one speaking with you is he." The man puts what he has understood from the tradition together with this continuing experience of Jesus and makes the judgment: "Lord, I believe." As judgments of fact and value raise questions for deliberation, so does the blind man decide and respond: "And he worshiped him" (9:35–38). His aggregation into Jesus' vision of reality is complete and the man healed provides the platform for Jesus' parting shot at those who do not see/understand. Some of the Pharisees ask yet another question about the literal level of reality, trapped as they are in fixed judgments about themselves: "Surely we are not blind, are we?" For them it is a rhetorical question: they have eyesight. But for the reader their spiritual blindness could not be more evident. Jesus has shown the dangers of their enslavement within a narrow horizon, and now he pointedly states the far deeper danger of egotistic refusal to acknowledge that bondage: "If you were blind, you would not have sin. But now that you say, 'We see,' your sin remains" (9:39–41).

Another image leads to another failure for some of the characters. Following the Good Shepherd discourse of 10:1–21, we find a series of questions that continue to show the intransigence that does not allow transformation as the divided "Jews" continue to argue. The first: "'He has a demon and is out of his mind. Why listen to him?' Others were saying, 'These are not the words of one who has a demon. Can a demon open the eyes of the blind?'" (10:20–21). In the second question, there seems to be something in the common fund of traditional knowledge that suggests that demons are not able to do such healing works, and the implied judgment offers a path to deliberation: if demons cannot open the eyes of the blind, there is now need to decide how to respond to Jesus. Yet there is no evidence that the next step is taken; the narrative suggests yet another dead end for some characters to a potentially fruitful question, one that the authorial audience can certainly answer correctly.

Immediately in the next scene (10:22–39), Jesus is accosted while walking in the temple during the Feast of Dedication: "How long will you keep us in suspense? If you are the Messiah, tell us plainly." The demand for something greater than all of the experiential evidence—what the Johannine Jesus has already said and done—is laughable in its obstinacy, as Jesus' reply indicates: "I have told you, and you do not believe." His brief soliloquy culminates in "I and the Father are One" (10:30) and leads those present to attempt again to stone him for blasphemy. Jesus then asks the rhetorical question, "Is it not written in your law, 'I said, you are gods?'" His exegesis of Psalm 82 pointedly explicates the rigidity that will not allow his opponents to incorporate either the experience of Jesus or of his good works, so that they cannot "know and understand"[17] the presence of God in their midst.

The Good Shepherd teachings serve as a setup for the sign that will embody the teaching: the raising of Lazarus (11:1–53). What initially could be heard as a disappointed accusation from

---

17. Moloney (*Gospel of John*, 321) points out that "the use of the aorist subjunctive here . . . denotes the beginning of knowledge and understanding at a point of time. This is Jesus' hope, and thus his exhortation."

Martha ("Lord, if you had been here, my brother would not have died") turns into an opportunity to express her inchoate faith: "But even now I know that God will give you whatever you ask of him" (11:22). Sensing an open door, Jesus continues to encourage her to think along the lines of life rather than death, including his identity as the resurrection and the life. His question to her, "do you believe this?" is met positively if incompletely.[18] Despite the progress with Martha, division continues among "the Jews," even after Jesus raises Lazarus (11:35–37, 45–46). That faction makes its final decision to put Jesus to death, so that Jesus' most poignant display of the divine *dynamis* causes the most tragic and erroneous answer to a question for deliberation in the gospel.

As the narrative transitions to Jerusalem, the questions for understanding become nearly depressing, given what the authorial audience has already learned about who Jesus is and where he is from through the story. The scene describing Jesus' return to the home of Martha, Mary, and Lazarus poses only the hostile question from Judas Iscariot about the wasting of the perfume (12:5), Jesus does not bother to redirect the question as he did in a comparable scene in Mark (14:6); rather, he simply scolds Judas to leave her alone, leaving a lingering feeling of doom in the audience for the fate of a Judas who clearly does not understand what he is experiencing in Jesus.

"We have heard from the law that the Messiah remains forever. How can you say that the Son of Man must be lifted up? Who is this Son of Man?" Jesus speaks again to a crowd, and his final answer to their question is carefully couched in the vocabulary of the prologue: following the light rather than the darkness. Despite the clarity and the signs, they do not believe (12:34–37). A curtain seems to be coming down on reasonable belief at this point in the gospel leading to Jesus death, and perhaps the hem of the curtain hits the stage floor when we read that "many, even of the authorities, believed in him. But because of the Pharisees they did not confess it, for fear that they would be put out of the synagogues; for they loved human glory more than the glory that comes from

---

18. Moloney, "Can Everyone Be Wrong?," 514–16.

God" (12:42–43). As we have seen earlier in the narrative (5:44), understanding—even correct understanding—is not enough for aggregation into God's glorious revelation of the true nature of reality: the question for deliberation must be asked and followed through successfully.

Jerusalem: Snapshots Return

While Jesus' final time with his disciples contains more snapshot questions for understanding, essentially to move a monologue along, they are of consequence in the body of teaching primarily to show that even at this point, the disciples are asking questions of topics that should already be understood. For example, Jesus asks after he washes the disciples' feet, "Do you know what I have done for you?" (13:12). Even though he seems to be asking for a judgment, his immediate move to an answer shows the question is rhetorical and serves primarily to highlight the need for them to be attentive and understand. Jesus' rather sharp exchanges of questions with Peter (13:36–38), Philip (14:8–14), and the group (16:16–19) underscore that the disciples are still reaching for better understanding to clarify the deliberations in which they will soon have to engage. The goal of Jesus' discourses here is to point the disciples repeatedly in the right direction for understanding, judgment, and deliberation: they will both believe and do great works (14:10–14). And at one point indeed, they think they've got it: "His disciples said, 'Yes, now you are speaking plainly, not in any figure of speech! Now we know that you know all things, and do not need to have anyone question you; by this we believe that you came from God'" (16:29–31). They are trying, and they have reached a significant judgment by finally understanding that yes, Jesus is from God. But then Jesus immediately says, "'Do you now believe? The hour is coming, and indeed it has come, when you will be scattered, each one to his home, and you will leave me alone'" (16:32). In other words, there is never a time when they *for their own sake* can stop asking questions; that they have stopped at this point allows Jesus to point out that their answers to the obvious question for deliberation, "what then should we do?" will be inadequate in the short run.

From this point until the death of Jesus, the questions are strategically located to reveal Jesus as essentially in control of events,[19] as the disciples correctly discerned, "knowing all things," and that he is the presence of the divine *dynamis*, having come from God. His double questioning ("whom are you looking for?") of the soldiers and police, for example, serves to display his foreknowledge and their recognition of the divine "I am" (18:4-9). His foreknowledge is again emphasized in the questions of the bystanders to Peter about his connection with Jesus (18:17, 25-26). The interaction with the high priest and one of the police continues to expose the intransigence of those who ask the same questions over and over because they simply refuse to see the power of God standing in front of them or to listen to his teachings (18:21-22). It is only left for the authentic power of Jesus and the mock and ineffectual power of the Roman government to play itself out in the scenes between Jesus and Pilate. Pilate alternates between questions for understanding (18:29, 33, 35b; 19:9), and sarcastic or hasty judgments with leading questions (18:35a, 37, 38, 39; 19:10). While various traits of Pilate's character are revealed by these questions, the trait that wins out in his final decision is selfishness, "thus fulfilling his judicial role in an unjust way . . . he opts to safeguard his own position instead of making any further attempt to set Jesus free."[20] Pilate manifests a type of block to understanding, reflection, and deliberation that we have seen before in the narrative (5:44; 12:42-43), but here we seen the tragic force of its danger. All of Pilate's failing questions are designed in the larger picture to display his lack of real power as he attempts to avoid crucifying Jesus, and hence the failure of worldly power that opposes God's plan for salvation. Pilate also cannot see what is in front of him, as his skepticism regarding truth sends the authorial audience back to the "world" of the prologue in which God's Word becomes flesh in Jesus, who is "full of grace and truth" (1:14).

19. Schnackenburg, *Gospel of John*, 3:270.
20. Tolmie, "Pontius Pilate," 594-95.

The Gospel of John

It is left for the questions in the resurrection scenes to underscore previous themes and to open snapshot views of growth in understanding of Jesus' identity. Mary's mourning the loss of Jesus is shown by questions and answers to be misguided. When the angels ask her, "Woman, why are you weeping," she focuses on not knowing where Jesus is. While the context suggests she is seeking Jesus' body, her words suggest she is seeking Jesus himself, like Jesus' early question to the two disciples of John the Baptist, what are you seeking? (1:38). That parallel is heightened by Jesus, who is in fact present, asking, "Woman, why are you weeping? Whom are you looking for?" (20:15). This time the question is not *what*; after all the explanations about who Jesus is throughout the gospel, it is clear that they are seeking a "whom." Mary "responds to his voice by 'coming to.' She recognizes her Rabbi, her shepherd who knows his sheep and calls them by name."[21] Her announcement to the disciples, "I have seen the Lord" (20:18), shows that she correctly asked and answered questions for judgment and deliberation: she is now more than a disciple; her knowledge and love has moved her to action, to witness. Through reasonable inquiry, despite beginning with a less than savvy question that shows "the darkness of unfaith (vv. 1–2, 11–15), she has passed through the conditioned faith that led her to recognize Jesus as her Rabbi (vv. 16–17a). She now announces that she has seen the risen Lord . . . Another foundational character from the earliest Christian community has journeyed from the darkness of unfaith through a partial faith into perfect belief."[22]

Jesus' final questions to the disciples during his resurrection appearances serve to help the authorial audience to observe both the growth in the disciples and the necessity of continued questioning to keep expanding their horizons. Thomas acknowledges "my Lord and my God" (a triumph of understanding), and Jesus' response, "have you believed because you have seen me? Blessed are those who have not seen and yet have come to believe" (20:28–29) detracts not at all from Thomas' confession but highlights the

---

21. Clark-Soles, "Mary Magdalene," 637.
22. Moloney, *Gospel of John*, 527.

necessity for belief that can't be confirmed by direct experience. Jesus' question "children, you have no fish, have you?" sets up another recognition of Jesus' identity and the reasonable faith in him, when the sudden abundance is interpreted as only made possible by the presence of the divine *dynamis* (21:5–7), as the disciples have seen before but not understood. And finally, Peter's triple redemption countering his triple denial brings him to clearer judgment than before and to a question for deliberation, essentially, will you feed my sheep? "'Very truly, I tell you, when you were younger, you used to fasten your own belt and to go wherever you wished. But when you grow old, you will stretch out your hands, and someone else will fasten a belt around you and take you where you do not wish to go.' (He said this to indicate the kind of death by which he would glorify God.)" After this "prediction" in which Jesus finally tells Peter what he *will* be able to do instead of what he *won't* be able to do, Jesus says "Follow me'" (John 21:18–19). Peter's response by following Jesus indicates that he finally understands more than the literal and acts on it: transformation.

Conclusion

The Fourth Gospel has somewhat different theological foci and literary strategies than does the Second, but the demonstration of the critical need for a successful questioning process to lead to transformation is remarkably similar in both. Both contain examples of a reasonable progression through the operations of understanding, judgment, and deliberation that leads to reasonable faith. The two gospels also have examples of such processes that are thwarted by an unreasonably tight hold on previous judgments despite new evidence that points toward expansion or even overturning of those judgments. While auditors both past and present of these gospels may chuckle or roll their eyes at the dullness of some of the characters, recognizing how the questioning process is somewhat similar to the "ritual process" of separation, liminality, and aggregation allows us to sympathize with how painful the movement through those processes can be and perhaps even to notice when we ourselves are caught in a comparable net of intransigence. In the next chapter, we will turn to the question of how these lessons learned in the Gospels of Mark and John may be transposed into our own search for reasonable faith.

4

After Easter

The Application

The goal of this chapter is to suggest principles for the application of the insights gleaned from the gospels of Mark and John to our contemporary spiritual search. We move through life, we learn, we make decisions in favor of the good, we act to achieve some good. The good could be a very simple, a vital good, like food and rest, or it could be a social, political or economic good. In other words, we are constantly in the process of *becoming* through self-transcendence. How do we make the process of becoming intentional rather than drift through life with little awareness of what we are making of ourselves? In what follows we will seek to elucidate more precisely the processes we have examined in two gospels in order to explore possible applications in the spiritual life.

The dramatic gospel narratives are not, of course, generalized theories of human self-transcendence; yet, artistic productions such as the literature of the New Testament do exemplify universal or transcendental human operations and processes. The characters in the gospels of Mark and John operate within symbolic narratives, and the authors have controlled their actions and implied their motivations. We know them only in so far as the author has drawn them. Regarding an application to a contemporary spiritual journey, the point is to place ourselves in the narratives to see what our response might be, could be, or should be. Rather than condemn or praise the characters, we enter into the narratives and analogously place ourselves in their situations for the sake of taking stock of our own spiritual journey. We pay attention to the symbolic narratives of the characters in the gospels to learn through the evangelists' art how to be disciples of Jesus. And the first question to ourselves is always, "Do you want to be made well?" (John 5:6).

Application is a much more flexible process than exegesis. When a biblical scholar is analyzing the data of the gospel texts, her interpretation is constrained by the words of the text, its literary style, and the social, religious and political contexts in which it was written. The exegete does not expect to pinpoint in a particular character a pure example of intellectual, moral or religious self-transcendence. Art moves us through our feelings, and so what we get from any religiously motivated reflection on the texts is personalized insight and affective exhortation, not clinical examples of a particular kind of self-transcendence or its failure. Lonergan and Turner have systematized basic human experiences and processes, processes we can discern through the texts narrating religious life in the ancient Mediterranean. The key question as put in ancient terms by Luke Johnson is: how does one gain access to the divine *dynamis* that many in the first century looked for in signs and wonders?

The necessary steps to an exercise of our full humanity are in Bernard Lonergan's terminology, "transcendental imperatives." These rules for authentic human living are transcendental because they transcend any culture, time, or place; they are imperatives because by being obedient to them we grow and develop as human beings. That growth heads toward the divine font of all being and love. In the gospel narratives the font or source of this drive toward self-transcendence, what Johnson calls the divine *dynamis*, is experienced by characters in the stories when they encounter Jesus. The narratives, as we have seen, also dramatize negative examples of this encounter. Both positive and negative examples point in the same direction: all are presented with the challenge to enter more fully into the divine order of things being renewed by Jesus.

Questioning, as we have seen in two gospels, is the engine of the process. As Lonergan points out, however, questions for understanding and for judgment lead us to a self-transcendence that is still "only cognitive." It is when we responsibly answer questions for deliberation that "self-transcendence becomes moral" as we ask about what is of objective value; and "because we can ask such questions, an answer them, and live by the answers, we can effect in our living a moral self-transcendence."[1]

The Precepts

The specific precepts that set us moving toward self-transcendence correspond to the basic structure of consciousness. We need to be attentive to experience, to be intelligent when seeking the meaning of that experience, to be reasonable when determining the truth of the meanings that our thinking proposes, to be responsible when acting on our judgments of fact and value, and finally to be in love with the ultimate source of existence. When we discern that we have failed to obey these precepts, the precepts call for repentance and change.

The first precept is *be attentive*. Attention and inattention are closely related to understanding and misunderstanding; one cannot understand if one is not paying attention. Paying attention, as those who practice any form of meditation know well, is the key to being present to one's fully human life, and yet it at times seems nearly impossible. Also in the first century as our texts have shown us, some characters allow their new encounter with Jesus to raise questions that produce new insight. They notice that something special, something wondrous and healing, is manifest especially in the acts of Jesus, "another order of reality invading and transfiguring the present. The miracles become symbols of that divine reality, making it realizable in the experience of those who encounter

---

1. Lonergan, *Method*, 104.

Jesus: those, in particular, whose lives are crushed by pain, oppression, and suffering."[2] The blind man Bartimaeus (Mark 10:46–52) paid attention to Jesus, understood the implications regarding the reign of God and wanted to be part of it while others tried to prevent him.

What often inhibits certain characters in the gospel narratives from attending to Jesus is a rigid imposition of prior understandings or images that block the characters' grasp of what is going on in the encounter. Recall the scene in the gospel of John when Jesus is confronted while walking in the temple during the Feast of Dedication by stubborn interlocutors: "How long will you keep us in suspense? If you are the Messiah, tell us plainly" (John 10:24). The precise point is that if they had been paying attention, they would have had their answer. Another example is the Jews' assertion that they are sons of Abraham and have never been enslaved (8:33). Not only have the sons and daughters of Abraham been enslaved more than once, the very characters in this scene are enslaved to their preconceptions. Watching characters in a narrative be that spirituality obtuse is amusing, but the humor has a point. It leads the reader to ask, when is our range of what serves as evidence so narrow as to make us obtuse to God's work right before our eyes? Although God's work in the gospel takes forms somewhat unfamiliar to these characters, there is enough that is familiar from the tradition to make clear whose work is being done. Like some characters in the gospels, we can refuse to pay attention to God's love manifest in Jesus when it does not conform to our preconceived formulas, patterns or habits.

We have been arguing that belief is an essential element in the acquisition of knowledge, and this knowledge is passed on in the form of tradition. But the common fund of knowledge—what has been passed down as heritage and accepted by belief—sometimes suffers from bias. Common nonsense can accompany traditional common sense. Distortions in our knowing caused by inattention, when it results in a failure of self-transcendence, goes by the religious name of sin. "Some of the Pharisees near him heard this

2. Lee, "Signs and Works," 101.

and said to him, 'Surely we are not blind, are we?' Jesus said to them, 'If you were blind, you would not have sin. But now that you say, "We see," your sin remains'" (John 9:40–41). Another example: Jesus' healing of the man with the withered hand brings only a murderous impulse out in those present who are threatened by the exposure of their hardness of heart (Mark 3:1–6).

The second precept is *be intelligent*. In other words, figure out what is going on. The people in the synagogue at Capernaum pay attention to the exorcism and ask themselves the next relevant question: "What is this?" and immediately find an intelligent answer: "A new teaching—with authority!" (Mark 1:27). On the other hand, the very sympathetic character of Nicodemus is indeed paying attention, and he is not applying some inherited standard in a rigid way that would block insight, yet he just does not get it. The rebirth that Jesus insisted on in his dialogue with Nicodemus was not a matter of returning to the womb nor of becoming someone other than Nicodemus. Jesus' encouragement was for the self to grow, develop, change through new understanding, conversion and discipleship. Self-transcendence can occur intellectually, morally, and religiously, but they are all forms of development in the human being. Intellectual self-transcendence occurs when, through learning, one has gone beyond what one was in some way and so is different as a result of that learning. When one knows something new, what Saint Paul calls the "old self," the one who was ignorant of what one has now learned, is transcended. Learning, in other words, is not a mere accumulation of facts but the self in transformation.

Nicodemus seems to be a "liminal" character throughout the gospel; his situation is ambiguous, a location beyond his inherited assumptions. But he has not come through to full understanding, let alone discipleship.[3] Although he does not understand the riddle about being born again, his second appearance later in the gospel shows him encouraging the Pharisees to give Jesus a fair

---

3. The liminal state is "neither here nor there; they are betwixt and between the positions assigned and arrayed by custom, convention, and ceremony" (Turner, *Ritual Process*, 94).

hearing. He seems to be reaching for understanding and certainly not actively hostile. Yet as the gospel begins drawing to a close, he is lugging a bag of spices to the tomb in order to anoint the body (19:39). He has not grasped the reality of the resurrection. Had he understood Jesus' riddle, Nicodemus might have shown a different moral response to the Pharisees' dismay that the Temple police have not arrested Jesus (7:51–52). After asking that Jesus be given a fair hearing, the Pharisees dismiss him by asking if he too is from Galilee, and Nicodemus once again disappears from the scene. When things get tough, he always evaporates. He stops short of what Lonergan calls "real self-transcendence," a deliberative move from knowledge to action for the good. Nicodemus' timid decision does not move him very far. His confusion and timidity demonstrate the connection between intellectual and moral self-transcendence, his failure to understand issues in a weak moral response to Jesus. The process of questioning moves the process of self-transcendence forward, but for Nicodemus, the restricted questions, remaining as they do on the literal level, soon stall the process.

Being intelligent requires tenacity, a tenacity sometimes enhanced by challenge. The Samaritan woman (John 4:1–42) persists in trying to understand Jesus' opaque riddles until her curiosity and persistence pay off, but that insight requires that she crash through some barriers set up by traditional, received judgments. In like manner, the man born blind (John 9:1–41) is pressed by the obstinate hostility and obstinacy of his questioners to move forward step by step toward the truth and discipleship. The father of the sick child tenaciously works through his own resistance (Mark 9:14–24).

But insight is not enough, as the next precept shows. We must also *be reasonable*, that is, seek verification. "Philip found Nathanael, and said to him, 'We have found him of whom Moses in the law and also the prophets wrote, Jesus of Nazareth, the son of Joseph.' Nathanael said to him, 'Can anything good come out of Nazareth?' Philip said to him, 'Come and see'" (John 1:45–46). Philip has proposed an idea: Jesus is the one whom Moses and the prophets identified. But is Jesus really that figure? Nathaniel's skepticism reflects the evangelist's use, as we have seen, of concern for a literal location as an impediment to discipleship. But his question also points up the need for verification: so you say, Philip, but are you right? Is your bright idea merely wishful thinking? Philip's response is to agree with Nathaniel's need for verification, and for that to happen, he needs to examine the evidence: Come and see.

A similar dynamic is at work in the story of the Samaritan woman at the well of Jacob. Many Samaritans came to believe in Jesus because of the woman's testimony, and so unlike Nathaniel they did not begin with skepticism, yet they also sought evidence and came to verify for themselves what they at first believed on testimony. "And many more believed because of his word. They said to the woman, 'It is no longer because of what you said that we believe, for we have heard for ourselves, and we know that this is truly the Savior of the world'" (John 4:39–42). The Samaritan villagers believe, seek and later see for themselves. Their belief allows them to know Jesus through a witness, but it also opens the possibility for verification and more direct encounter. Faith and reason operate in this example toward mutual support.

In the Markan story of the man with the sick son, the father "immediately" has the insight that he should try to get Jesus to help. The disciples have been unable to cast out the spirit that is causing what sounds like epilepsy in the boy. The father asks Jesus to help "if he is able," a conditional attitude that annoys Jesus, who retorts, "'If you are able!—All things can be done for the one who believes.'" Once again belief is promoted as the starting point but not at the expense of reason, and so the father asks for help with the verification: "I believe, help my unbelief" (Mark 9:23–24). The father knows that his doubts must be overridden—he must believe—in order for his boy to have a chance for healing. Belief in this context is the most rational response.

More than correctly figuring it out, the drive toward self-transcendence requires that we *be responsible*. Judgments of fact and judgments of value move us to make a decision and to do something about what we know and value. In the context of the gospel narratives, if Jesus is the messiah, the characters are challenged to recognize the fact and get on board. The messiah brings God's order, and so we too need to take our respective places and play our role in it. Ideally we would all respond as disciples as quickly as Bartimaeus did. It is more likely, however, that most of us follow the slow but steady path of the man born blind or the father with the sick child (help my unbelief!), with a few irritating nudges from both our friends and our enemies along the way.

At the core of the drive toward self-transcendence, as its source and goal, is God's love. The precept *be in love* is the call to religious conversion, to being in love with God. But it is not a call concerned in the first place with human achievement. Rather, being in love with God is God's gift. When you are being intelligent, you grasp what is going on; when you are in love, you find yourself being grasped by the unconditional love that transforms your prior horizon and transvalues your previous values. When it happens, as Lonergan puts it, "then there is a new basis for all valuing and all doing good. In no way are fruits of intellectual or moral conversion negated or diminished. On the contrary, all human pursuit of the true and the good is included within and furthered by a cosmic context and purpose and, as well, there now accrues to man the power of love to enable him to accept the suffering involved in undoing the effects of decline."[4] The state of being-in-love (religious self-transcendence) manifests itself when one acts not simply for a particular good but for the sake of one's love of the source of all goodness. In the gospel narratives, the characters who encounter the divine *dynamis*, grasped by the love that Jesus embodies, are moved to think and decide and act in a new way. In other words, lest we imagine that the direction of the development is only one way, from intellectual to moral to religious, there is also development in the opposite direction from religious to moral and intellectual. So when one is in love with God, one makes different moral decisions and one is open to understanding more than one could have understood prior to being in love with God. "From a causal viewpoint," Lonergan says, "one would say that first there is

4. Lonergan, *Method*, 242.

God's gift of his love."[5] The call of the disciples in Mark is emblematic of this religious falling in love. How else do we explain the immediate response of these men?

> As Jesus passed along the Sea of Galilee, he saw Simon and his brother Andrew casting a net into the lake—for they were fishermen. And Jesus said to them, 'Follow me and I will make you fish for people.' And immediately they left their nets and followed him. As he went a little farther, he saw James son of Zebedee and his brother John, who were in their boat mending the nets. Immediately he called them; and they left their father Zebedee in the boat with the hired men, and followed him. (Mark 1:16–20)

Three aspects of this passage suggest a transvaluation of these men's values when they respond to the call to become disciples. First, they respond immediately to Jesus. When Jesus calls them the repetition of the word "immediately" suggests that some sudden and unexpressed desire or attraction initiates an urgency for intellectual and moral questioning. They do not listen to a speech or witness a sign and only then consider the implications before acting. Second, they are leaving their way of making a living. In the case of the sons of Zebedee the text indicates that they are leaving comfortable material conditions: their father's fishing business is prosperous enough to have hired extra help. Finally, James and John are acting in a way that can only be construed as insulting to their father. Something has happened to them that has radically changed their horizons. People in all times and places fall in love with God and when that happens, everything changes. John Wesley's heart, for example, was "strangely warmed" at Aldersgate, and this experience eventually led to his "General Rules" (1742): do no harm, do good, stay in love with God. Falling in love does not mean that no mistakes are ever made again. "The narrator [of Mark, but it could just as well apply to John] has depicted the disciples as afraid, with little faith or understanding, concerned to

---

5. Lonergan, *Method*, 243.

save their own lies, and preoccupied with their own importance, but, nonetheless, leaving all and persevering in following Jesus."[6]

The significant questioning of the disciples in Mark, while often not on target, comes out of a prior love or desire for what Jesus is teaching and embodying. The liberation that the characters in the gospels seek is initiated in a faith born of love. "It is not propaganda and it is not argument but religious faith that will liberate human reasonableness from its ideological prisons."[7] Lonergan is here articulating a relationship between faith and reason that runs counter to the kind of rationalism that we have criticized briefly in the first chapter. We have shown in previous chapters how the gospels dramatize this relationship whereby faith liberates reason through the importance of both the successes and failures of the questioning process.

Love initiates the process but discipleship is a lifelong effort that requires continual care; the achievement is never complete. The concluding chapter of John's gospel returns to Peter's discipleship, which has had its ups and downs:

> "Very truly, I tell you, when you were younger, you used to fasten your own belt and to go wherever you wished. But when you grow old, you will stretch out your hands, and someone else will fasten a belt around you and take you where you do not wish to go." (He said this to indicate the kind of death by which he would glorify God.) After this he said to him, "Follow me." (John 21:18–19)

One would not want to suggest that self-transcendence is easily or quickly accomplished. In the first chapter we suggested that the process of understanding, judgment, and deliberation are similar to the ritual process of separation, liminality, and aggregation, a process not without the pain and fear of loss, uncertainty, and change. As Tannehill wisely remarks on discipleship and the passion in the Gospel of Mark:

---

6. Rhoads et al., *Mark as Story*, 129.
7. Lonergan, *Method*, 117.

> The passion of Jesus, in its Markan meaning, is not a solution to problems of discipleship but presents the problem in its sharpest form. Following the crucified Jesus means taking up the cross oneself (8:34). It also means becoming slave of all (10:44). These are not demands that disappear after Easter (see the prediction of suffering in 13:9–13) nor do they suddenly become easy to fulfill. Even in the first half of the Gospel the blindness of the disciples is associated with fear, lack of trust, and anxious self- concern (see 4:40–41, 6:49–52, 8:14–18), problems which do not disappear in the post-Easter church. Nor does the message of the resurrection guarantee a faithful response. The disciples heard this message from Jesus beginning at 8:31, yet failed to follow him, and an indication of further failure by Jesus' followers (16:8) comes immediately after the resurrection message at the tomb. The decision of the author to write a Gospel, including the story of the first disciples, rests on the assumption that there are essential similarities between the situation of these disciples and the situation of the early church, so that, in telling a story about the past, the author can also speak to his present.[8]

Serious self-examination is called for: when am I refusing to separate from the common sense that I have come to understand is common nonsense, or inadequate to experience in some way? When do I pull back before or during liminality for fear of isolation and rejection by the community? When do I fail to take the final step of aggregation, for which the question for deliberation is necessary? When am I holding on so rigidly to a belief or practice that I cannot see elements of a new life, or new way of thinking about traditional truth, that is right in front of me? If "the Son of Man is lord even of the Sabbath" (Mark 2:28) then discipleship will sometimes require that I separate myself from practices and assumptions that might even be closely associated with the handing on of the gospel in order to grasp a more pressing insight.

---

8. Tannehill, "Disciples in Mark," 393.

Focus upon the sacred (whether persons, buildings, objects, or texts) in a sense that sets them "apart" in an absolute way runs counter to the sacramental principle that is fundamental to Christianity, especially as a legacy of the Fourth Gospel. The sacred points to the "divine depth," the presence of the divine in physical reality as a whole. Jesus' action in the temple, in line with the prophetic traditions of Israel and especially in fulfillment of Zechariah 14:20–21, challenges all religious practice that absolutizes and consigns the presence and revelation of God simply to the realm of the sacred. When the Word became flesh and dwelt among us, while remaining ever in the bosom of the Father (1:14, 18), he pointed to the presence of God in the everyday and ordinary—as at Cana—as well as in the sacred and set apart.[9]

Rather than take people out of "this world," the divine *dynamis* directs them toward a deeper experience of God's intended cosmic order. The gospel stories function to bring their audiences into their role as one of the key drivers toward this cosmic order. One way Jesus' message is intended to be discovered through the questioning process that leads to self-transcendence of the human person, and self-transcending human beings are key drivers in bringing about the kingdom of God.

---

9. Byrne, *Life Abounding Abounding*, 63.

Conclusion

It is easy to get the relationship between faith and reason wrong. There is a tendency to unbalance the relationship by either reducing faith to a conclusion of reason or of giving no place to reason within the act of faith. The reality is subtler and more important. A fresh reading of the gospels, with attention given to the questions and answers that emerge in the interactions among the characters, and especially their encounters with Jesus, reveals that an accurate account of the relationship between thinking and believing presents faith as an act of reason while reason is understood as needing faith in order to be liberated from narrow horizons. When faith operates within the context of faith, self-transcendence is possible.

"Faith is the knowledge born of religious love."[1] In the first century, people were initially drawn to listen to Jesus for various reasons: curiosity, fear, the need for healing or simply a basic but indefinable yearning or desire. As depicted in the gospels of Mark and John, the characters frequently manifest this desire by asking questions. The answers they got, if they understood them, sometimes moved them forward to moral and religious transformation. At other times, they were stymied along the way by the inability or unwillingness to let go of previous, comfortable positions.

Why did some who encountered Jesus of Nazareth respond positively to him, accepting the risk so that their deepest desires could be met, while others used their inherited knowledge to

1. Lonergan, *Method*, 115.

Conclusion

resist what was new in Jesus? Within tradition itself, as part of the religious inheritance of Judaism, was a longstanding interplay between faith and reason. One need not look long into the Hebrew Bible to notice the kind of questioning of God and others that intends to move characters and readers to a deeper understanding of their relationships with God. The psalms are of course an obvious example, but the importance of questions for the purpose of reinterpretation of the tradition was essential to Jewish life at the time of Jesus, especially among the various kinds of Pharisees, whose synagogues were places of religious instruction as well as prayer.

Throughout this book, two extremes have been rejected: the notion that early Christianity promoted blind faith without reason and the claim that reason can operate fruitfully outside of any willingness to believe. If we read the ancient gospels carefully we will notice that the characters who encounter Jesus will make progress in understanding (and in many cases, in their physical healing) when they have faith. The response of faith is legitimated in ways that fit the context of first-century Judaism and some of these legitimations are different from our own. Still, no matter the context, what remains constant is the structure whereby belief makes knowledge possible and faith is most fruitful when there the reasons for belief are known.

Today it is still true that faith enables reason. But an uncritical faith—a credulity or an unthinking belief that clings to certitude at the expense of understanding—can undermine faith itself and at least slow down the response to the grace of ongoing conversion. Tradition as inherited knowledge can be an ambiguous treasure. On the one hand, without a willingness to have faith in what one inherits, reason would be sent back to an impossible starting point; reason without belief is humanly impossible. On the other hand, when the reasons for belief are disregarded, one is left without a way of differentiating between faith and prejudice. The well-known scene at Caesarea Philippi when Jesus asks the disciples, "Who do people say that I am," reveals the difference between faith and prejudice. The judgment that Peter has already made—the certitude that he shows when he rebukes Jesus for announcing his future suffering—must be broken down before Peter can move forward in his understanding of Jesus and his mission. Peter's skepticism here evokes great sympathy from the reader: not only does Peter not want to see his friend suffer, he also has scriptural reasons for thinking that the Messiah will be more ruler than sufferer. Yet Peter's prepackaged image of the Messiah blocks his insight into the new reality that Jesus represents. The scene exemplifies the case of one whose faith in a certitude—the Messiah will not suffer—must be challenged by reason. That in itself is not a condemnation of Peter, who is in the self-correcting process of learning in which mistakes are inevitable. Avoiding mistakes is only possible if we avoid the search. Pope Francis makes the point:

> In this quest to seek and find God in all things there is still an area of uncertainty. There must be. If a person says that he met God with total certainty and is not touched by a margin of uncertainty, then this is not good. For me, this is an important key. If one has the answers to all the questions—that is the proof that God is not with him. It means that he is a false prophet using religion for himself. The great leaders of the people of God, like Moses, have always left room for doubt. You must leave room for the Lord, not for our certainties; we must be humble. Uncertainty is in every true discernment that is open to finding confirmation in spiritual consolation.[2]

As the lives of most of Jesus' closest followers show after his death and resurrection, patience, tenacity, and the willingness to move on after mistakes puts us in a position of "helping to change the world from our nightmare into God's dream."[3]

---

2. Spadaro, "A Big Heart."
3. Curry, "General Convention."

Bibliography

Achtemeier, Paul J. *Mark*. Proclamation Commentaries. Philadelphia: Fortress, 1986.

Ando, Clifford. *Roman Religion*. Edinburgh Readings on the Ancient World. Edinburgh: Edinburgh University Press, 2003.

———. *The Matter of the Gods: Religion and the Roman Empire*. Transformation of the Classical Heritage 44. Berkeley: University of California Press, 2009.

Aristotle. *De Anima*. In *The Basic Works of Aristotle*. edited by Richard McKeon, 535–603. New York: Random House, 1941.

Berger, Peter L. *The Sacred Canopy: Elements of a Sociological Theory of Religion*. Garden City, NY: Doubleday, 1969.

Berger, Peter L., and Thomas Luckmann. *The Social Construction of Reality: A Treatise in the Sociology of Knowledge*. Garden City, NY: Doubleday, 1967.

Brawley, Robert L. *Luke–Acts and the Jews: Conflict, Apology, and Conciliation*. Society of Biblical Literature Monograph Series 33. Atlanta: Scholars, 1987.

Brown, Raymond E. *The Gospel according to John*. Anchor Bile 29, 29A. Garden City, NY: Doubleday, 1966–1970.

Burge, Gary M. *John*. NIV Application Commentary. Grand Rapids: Zondervan, 2000.

Byrne, Brendan. *Life Abounding: A Reading of John's Gospel*. Collegeville, MN: Liturgical Press, 2014.

Carson, D. A. *The Gospel according to John*. Grand Rapids: Baker, 1984.

Clark-Soles, Jaime. "Mary Magdalene." In *Character Studies in the Fourth Gospel: Narrative Approaches to Seventy Figures in John,* edited by Steven A. Hunt et al., 626–40. Wissenschaftliche Untersuchungen zum Neuen Testament 314. Tübingen: Mohr/Siebeck, 2013.

Crowe, Frederick E. *Theology of the Christian Word: A Study in History*. Mahwah, NJ: Paulist, 1978.

Curry, Michael. General Convention Sermon 2012. https://www.youtube.com/watch?v=abJMKeyCWoQ.

Bibliography

Dewey, Joanna. "The Survival of Mark's Gospel: A Good Story?" *Journal of Biblical Literature* 123 (2004) 495–507.

Donahue, John R. *The Gospel of Mark.* Sacra Pagina 2. Collegeville, MN: Liturgical, 2002.

Dowd, Sharyn, and Elizabeth Struthers Malbon. "The Significance of Jesus' Death in Mark: Narrative Context and Authorial Audience." *Journal of Biblical Literature* 125 (2006) 270–97.

Dwyer, Timothy. *The Motif of Wonder in the Gospel of Mark.* Journal for the Study of the New Testament. Supplement Series 128. Sheffield: Sheffield Academic, 1996.

Giblin, C. H. "Suggestion, Negative Response, and Positive Action in St. John's Gospel (John 2:1–11; 4:46–54; 7:2–14; 11:1–44)." *New Testament Studies* 26 (1979–1980) 197–211.

Guijarro, Santiago. "Why Does the Gospel of Mark Begin as It Does?" *Biblical Theology Bulletin* 33 (2003) 28–38.

Hare, Douglas R. A. *Mark.* Westminster Bible Companion. Louisville: Westminster John Knox, 1996.

Heitmüller, Wilhelm. *Das Johannes-Evangelium, die Johannes-Briefe und die Offenbarung des Johannes.* Schriften des Neuen Testament 4. Göttingen: Vandenhoeck & Ruprecht, 1920.

Hunt, Steven A. et al., eds. *Character Studies in the Fourth Gospel: Narrative Approaches to Seventy Figures in John.* Wissenschaftliche Untersuchungen zum Neuen Testament 314. Tübingen: Mohr/Siebeck, 2013.

Igboin, Benson O. "Bias and Conversion: An Evaluation of Spiritual Transformation." *Evangelical Review of Theology* 37 (2013) 166–82.

Jinkins, Michael and Stephen Breck Reid. "God's Forsakenness: The Cry of Dereliction as an Utterance Within the Trinity." *Horizons in Biblical Theology* 19 (1997) 33–57.

Johnson, Luke Timothy. *Among the Gentiles: Greco-Roman Religion and Christianity.* New Haven: Yale University Press, 2009.

———. *Religious Experience in Earliest Christianity: A Missing Dimension in New Testament Studies.* Minneapolis: Fortress, 1998.

———. "Transformation of the Mind and Moral Discernment in Paul." In *Early Christianity and Classical Culture: Studies in Honor of Abraham J. Malherbe*, edited by John T. Fitzgerald et al., 215–36. Novum Testamentum Supplements 110. Leiden: Brill, 2003.

Keener, Craig S. *The Gospel of John: A Commentary.* 2 vols. Peabody, MA: Hendrickson, 2003.

Kim, Yung Suk. *A Transformative Reading of the Bible: Explorations of Holistic Human Transformation.* Eugene, OR: Cascade, 2013.

Labahn, Michael. "The Parents of the Man Born Blind: The Reason for Fear without True Reason." In *Character Studies in the Fourth Gospel: Narrative Approaches to Seventy Figures in John*, edited by Steven A. Hunt et al., 447–50. Wissenschaftliche Untersuchungen zum Neuen Testament 314. Tübingen: Mohr/Siebeck, 2013.

Lee, Dorothy A. "'Signs and Works': The Miracles in the Gospels of Mark and John." *Colloquium* 47 (2015) 89–101.
Légasse, Simon *L'Évangile e Marc*. Lectio Divina Commentaires 5. 2 vols. Paris: Cerf, 1997.
Locke, John. *An Essay Concerning Human Understanding*. http://www.earlymoderntexts.com/assets/pdfs/locke1690book1.pdf
Lonergan, Bernard J. F. *Insight: A Study of Human Understanding*. San Francisco: Harper & Row, 1957.
———. *Method in Theology*. New York: Crossroad, 1972.
———. "The Subject." *A Second Collection*, edited by William F. J. Ryan and Bernard J. Tyrell, 69–86. Philadelphia: Westminster, 1974.
Marcus, Joel. *Mark: A New Translation with Introduction and Commentary*. Anchor Bible 27. New York: Doubleday, 2000–2008.
McCarthy, Gerald D. *The Ethics of Belief Debate*. AAR Studies in Religion 41. Atlanta: Scholars, 1986.
McVann Mark. "The Passover in Mark: Transformation Ritual." *Biblical Theology Bulletin* 18 (1988) 96–101.
Moloney, Francis J. "Can Everyone Be Wrong? A Reading of John 11.1—12.8." *New Testament Studies* 49 (2003) 505–27.
———. *The Gospel of John*. Sacra Pagina 4. Collegeville, MN: Liturgical, 1998.
———. "Mark 6:6–30: Mission, The Baptist, and Failure." *Catholic Biblical Quarterly* 63 (2001) 647–63.
Newman, John Henry. *Grammar of Assent*. Garden City, NY: Doubleday, 1955.
———. "The Nature of Faith in Relation to Reason." *Oxford University Sermons* 11. London: SPCK, 1970.
Rabinowitz, Peter J. "Whirl without End: Audience-Oriented Criticism." *Contemporary Literary Theory*, edited by G. Douglas Atkins and Laura Morrow, 81–100. Amherst: University of Massachusetts Press, 1989.
Rhoads, David et al. *Mark as Story: An Introduction to the Narrative of a Gospel*. 2nd ed. Minneapolis: Fortress, 1999.
Rives, James B. *Religion in the Roman Empire*. Malden, MA: Blackwell, 2007.
Santos, Narry F. *Slave of All: The Paradox of Authority and Servanthood in the Gospel of Mark*. Journal for the Study of the New Testament Supplement Series 237. London: Sheffield Academic, 2003.
Schnackenburg, Rudolf. *The Gospel according to St. John*. 3 vols. Herders theological Commentary on the New Testament. Translated by Kevin Smyth. New York: Crossroad, 1968–82.
Spadaro, Antonio. "A Big Heart Open to God: The Exclusive Interview with Pope Francis." *America* (2013). http://www.americamagazine.org/pope-interview/.
Talbert, Charles H. *Reading John: A Literary and Theological Commentary on the Fourth Gospel and the Johannine Epistles*. New York: Crossroad, 1992.
Tannehill, Robert C. "The Disciples in Mark: The Function of a Narrative Role." *Journal of Religion* 57 (1977) 386–405.

Bibliography

Telford, W. R. *The Theology of the Gospel of Mark*. New Testament Theology. Cambridge: Cambridge University Press, 1999.

Thompson, Marianne Meye. *The Incarnate Word: Perspectives on Jesus in the Fourth Gospel*. Peabody, MA: Hendrickson, 1988.

Tolbert, Mary Ann. "How the Gospel of Mark Builds Character." *Interpretation* 47 (1993) 347–57.

Tolmie, D. Francois. "Pontius Pilate." In *Character Studies in the Fourth Gospel: Narrative Approaches to Seventy Figures in John*, edited by Steven A. Hunt et al., 78–97. Wissenschaftliche Untersuchungen zum Neuen Testament 314. Tübingen: Mohr/Siebeck, 2013.

Turner, Victor W. *The Ritual Process: Structure and Anti-Structure*. Ithaca, NY: Cornell University Press, 1969.

Wach, Joachim. "The Nature of Religious Experience." In *The Comparative Study of Religions*, edited by Joseph M. Kitagawa, 27–58. New York: Columbia University Press, 1958.

Williams, Joel F. *Other Followers of Jesus: Minor Characters as Major Figures in Mark's Gospel*. Journal for the Study of the New Testament Supplements 102. Sheffield: JSOT Press, 1994.

Witherington, Ben, III. *The Gospel of Mark. A Socio-Rhetorical Commentary*. Grand Rapids: Eerdmans, 2001.

Zimmerman, Ruben. "'The Jews': Unreliable Figures or Unreliable Narration?" In *Character Studies in the Fourth Gospel: Narrative Approaches to Seventy Figures in John*, edited by Steven A. Hunt et al., 71–109. Wissenschaftliche Untersuchungen zum Neuen Testament 314. Tübingen: Mohr/Siebeck, 2013.

www.ingramcontent.com/pod-product-compliance
Lightning Source LLC
Chambersburg PA
CBHW072011090426
42734CB00033B/2420